Housing and Health

The role of primary care

Edi

Par

Fore

Dav

Radcliffe

...cliffe Medical Press Ltd
18 Marcham Road
Abingdon
Oxon OX14 1AA
United Kingdom

www.radcliffe-oxford.com
The Radcliffe Medical Press electronic catalogue and online ordering facility. Direct sales to anywhere in the world.

British Library Cataloguing in Publication Data

A catalogue record for this book is available from the British Library.

ISBN 1 85775 948 6

Typeset by Action Publishing Technology Limited, Gloucester
Printed and bound by TJ International Ltd, Padstow, Cornwall

Contents

Foreword   v

Preface   vii

List of contributors   viii

1   Housing policy and health in Britain   1

Donna Easterlow and Susan J Smith

2   Housing conditions and health consequences   17

Jane Hopton, Stephen Platt and Linda Macleod

3   Homelessness and health: the role of primary care   47

Helen Lester

4   Ethnic minority health and housing   67

Mark RD Johnson and Richard Tomlins

5   Collaboration for meeting housing needs   79

Murray Hawtin

6   The primary care response   99

Adrian Hastings

7   Conclusion   109

Gilles de Wildt, Paramjit S Gill and Iona Heath

Index   117

Foreword

It can be one of those heartsink moments of general practice. Your patient looks at you pleadingly and utters those inevitable words 'Can I have a letter for the housing?', and, with an air of resignation, you agree.

But it needn't be like this. After all, every general practitioner is all too aware of how important social factors such as diet, education and housing can be to the health of our patients. We offer our advice and our prescriptions, but when our patients live in substandard housing our efforts seem to be doomed to produce only the most marginal success. Ten-minute consultations may be important, but they fade into insignificance compared to the many hours our patients spend in cold, damp, cramped, inadequate housing in demoralised and demoralising estates.

This timely guide to the role of primary care in the important area of housing and health will give us all reasons to stop and think. Even though I must have written hundreds of 'letters for the housing', I had never actually thought of rehousing as being a positively therapeutic act until I read this book – but of course it is. After all, there is a very real logic in awarding priority to those people in the housing queue who have significant health problems, as these are the very real people who will benefit the most.

It may be an inevitable truth of modern society that the housing market responds much more to the ability of a purchaser to pay rather than to their need, but in the area of social housing GPs can have a genuine impact. In addition, primary care trusts now have a public health function, and there can be few more important aspects of public health than inadequate housing. This publication presents the very considerable evidence base for the very clear link between housing and health, and also reviews the dreadful effects of homelessness. Research shows all too clearly that primary care services are almost always less available to the homeless, which means that this most needy of groups is the one to get the least health promotion. The inverse care law strikes again.

The RCGP seeks to encourage, foster and maintain the highest possible standards in general medical practice. This focus on the housing needs of our patients, and the health disaster that homelessness and inadequate housing represent, can begin to help us make a difference.

David Haslam
Chairman of Council
Royal College of General Practitioners
September 2002

Preface

Housing is an important determinant of health. A number of statutory and voluntary organisations are involved in providing access to good quality housing. Yet, professionals in these disparate organisations are not sure of each other's roles and responsibilities.

In June 1999, the Royal College of General Practitioners, in collaboration with the Chartered Institute of Housing, organised a conference that aimed to share ideas, experiences and visions to providing healthy housing for all. Some of the chapters in this book arose from presentations at that conference.

We hope the book will be of interest to all professionals involved with housing. It provides an overview of the impact of housing policy; the evidence base of the effect of housing on health; issues around homelessness; ethnic minority health and housing; collaborating with other organisations in delivering housing; and the role of the primary care teams as part of the new primary care trusts.

Paramjit S Gill
Gilles de Wildt
September 2002

List of contributors

Donna Easterlow
Lecturer, Department of Geography, University of Edinburgh

Paramjit S Gill
General Practitioner
Clinical Senior Lecturer, Department of Primary Care and General Practice, University of Birmingham

Adrian Hastings
General Practitioner
Senior Lecturer in Medical Education, Department of General Practice and Primary Health Care, University of Leicester

Murray Hawtin
Senior Policy Analyst, Policy Research Institute, Leeds Metropolitan University

Iona Heath
General Practitioner and Chair of the Health Inequalities Standing Group, Royal College of General Practitioners

Jane Hopton
Research Psychologist, Department of Community Health Sciences, University of Edinburgh

Mark RD Johnson
Professor, Mary Seacole Research Centre, De Montfort University, Leicester

Helen Lester
General Practitioner
Senior Lecturer, Department of Primary Care and General Practice, University of Birmingham

Linda Macleod
Research Fellow, Department of Sociology, Queen Margaret University College, Edinburgh

Stephen Platt
Professor, Research Unit in Health, Behaviour and Change, University of Edinburgh

Susan J Smith
Professor, Department of Geography, University of Edinburgh

Richard Tomlins
Professor, Race and Ethnic Diversity Research and Policy Partnership, Faculty of Business and Law, De Montfort University, Leicester

Gilles de Wildt
General Practitioner, Birmingham

Chapter 1

Housing policy and health in Britain

Donna Easterlow and Susan J Smith

Introduction

For over a century, housing policy in Britain has had a health dimension. This dimension has not always been explicit, and it has rarely been at the top of the policy agenda. Sometimes an emphasis on healthy housing has been deliberate, on other occasions inadvertent. Nevertheless, Britain is probably unique in the extent to which health needs have shaped housing interventions, and in the extent to which housing interventions have impinged on public health.

There are two broad ways in which housing policy and health interact. On the one hand, *housing policy is a powerful tool for regulating the built environment*. It is a way of managing the risk to health posed by damp, cold dwellings, a way of tackling homes which are disabling or in poor repair, a way of 'treating' unhealthy living environments. On the other hand, *housing interventions can affect where people live*. Housing policy can steer vulnerable people away from risky neighbourhoods; it can ensure that people with health problems secure housing appropriate to their needs.

The extent to which housing policy has been geared to health aims has varied through time and any success in using housing as a health intervention has been geographically uneven. These fluctuations and variations reflect the changing priorities built into housing policy which, after all, is variously about economic management, environmental regeneration and social policy.[1] For housing to achieve health gains, it is the social dimension that is most critical. In the last two decades, however, the social aims of housing policy have often been eclipsed by priorities rooted in the marketplace. It is against this background that we review the problems and potential associated with the two key means of using housing interventions to meet public health goals. First, we consider policies designed to secure a healthy stock of housing; second, we examine the policies which steer people with health problems into more or less therapeutic housing environments.

A quest for healthy housing

The pursuit of a healthy housing stock lay at the core of the earliest Public Health Acts in the late nineteenth century. At a time when infectious diseases still accounted for the majority of the death rate, and despite the lack of hard evidence to link poor housing with high risks, politicians made the regulation of housing environments their main health priority. This strategy paid off. Broad-based public health initiatives are generally agreed to be at least as important as clinical medicine in achieving the remarkable mortality transition that Britain experienced in the late nineteenth and early twentieth centuries.[2]

With time, however, the links between health and housing policy became less and less explicit. The last very dramatic intervention in the housing environment came with the slum clearances of the 1960s. By this time it was passively assumed rather than actively planned that by demolishing the worst of the slums and providing new, healthier replacement homes, the country would rid itself once and for all of its stock of unhealthy housing.

During the 1970s, however, and more so during the 1980s, complacency was replaced with concern. First, it was noted that high rise alternatives to the old city centre slums carried their own risks, particularly to mental health. Then the extent of disrepair and degradation in low income owner occupation, as well as in the newer but poorly built council stock, became evident, as did the health consequences of this. The most recent housing condition surveys in England, Scotland and Wales suggest that, against a background of cuts of 60% in public investment in housing, households in every tenure sector are subject to living conditions that may be harmful to their health.[3,4]

In response to some of these problems, and in the wake of a growing literature documenting the adverse health consequences of poor housing (*see* Chapter 2), recent rounds of legislation have recognised the health gains that might be secured from a number of policy arenas with potential to promote therapeutic environments. This legislation has generally emphasised the importance of national and local housing policy as one, perhaps the central, element of this. Ironically though, it is health rather than housing policy that has spearheaded this approach.

The relevance of housing to health policy

A key theme of *health* policy over the last decade or so has been a commitment both to tackling the root causes of ill health and promoting the quality of life of chronically sick and disabled people and others with care needs. In practice, this has largely revolved around reducing the role of the statutory health and social services in promoting the nation's health and in providing for its health and social care. Instead, health policy urges a wide range of organisations to share this responsibility; public health strategies now hinge on promoting 'healthy' public policies, inter-sectoral alliances and community care, all of which have housing at their core.

Two important public health documents – the Conservative's *Health of the Nation*[5] and Labour's *Saving Lives: our healthier nation*[6] – thus recognise that the causes of poor health and wellbeing include social and environmental factors as well as individual behaviour. While both documents make much of the importance of individuals adopting healthy lifestyles, the creation of healthy living and working environments is also a central concern. To this end, a range of local organisations spanning the public, private and voluntary sectors, both within and outwith the health domain, are encouraged to work together, and with government, under a 'new contract for health'. A range of initiatives, including health action zones (HAZs), health improvement programmes (HImPs), health impact assessments (HIAs) and joint funding arrangements have been introduced to encourage and provide the framework for this partnership approach. The public health function of government is similarly reflected in the idea to appraise all government policy for its effect on public health and in the appointment, for the first time, of a minister for public health in England whose specific responsibility is to co-ordinate health-promoting policy across government departments. All the surrounding discourse recognises that good quality housing has important beneficial impacts on health. Accordingly, both documents identify improvements to the nation's housing as a key to promoting good health, and as a common cause for which organisations and government can work together.

Concerning health and social care, the current government, through its upcoming *Supporting People* programme,[7] has continued the commitment of its Conservative predecessor to promoting the independence and wellbeing of people with a range of support and care needs through strategies of community care. These have been, and continue to be, predicated on the assumption that most people want to live in their own homes, and that care should be delivered to them there. To the extent that community care largely revolves around care in the home, it also relies on the availability of good quality, suitable, enabling dwellings. Policy documents concerned with community care and the delivery of support services recognise the 'crucial role housing has to play in community care' and call for health and social services to work closely with local housing authorities, housing associations and other providers of housing.[7,8]

The importance of good housing in promoting good health is thus recognised once again in the health policy sphere, as is the idea that health gains might be regarded as a legitimate objective for housing policy. The challenge now is to see housing policy respond.

The relevance of housing policy to health

There are some grounds for optimism here. The Government states that the objective of its housing policy is to offer everyone the opportunity of a decent home in order to promote, among other things, wellbeing and self-dependence, and to 'make a significant contribution to other policy objectives, for example, improving public health'.[9,10] Thus a range of initiatives has been introduced or expanded in order to promote the healthiness of the housing stock overall and to ensure decent housing conditions for vulnerable people, including the sick and disabled and those most at risk of ill health, largely those on low incomes. Many of these are discussed in the public health white paper,[6] acknowledging their particular contribution to its aims.

The suite of healthy housing policies on offer ranges from those which aim to tackle the problem at as early a stage as possible, i.e. at the point of housing construction, to others which seek to remedy the poor conditions of large parts of the existing housing stock. Building Regulations, for instance, are designed to safeguard the health and safety of people in and around buildings, including homes, by providing functional requirements for building design and construction. Several of the parts of the regulations (covering sound insulation, energy efficiency, drainage, fire safety, etc.) are currently under review with a view to improving standards of home building. Further, in a bid to improve the suitability, in particular the accessibility, of the housing stock for people with physical disabilities and mobility needs, Part M of the Building Regulations (covering access and facilities for disabled people) has already been extended (in 1999) to include all new homes.[10] The government is, however, encouraging builders to go even further than the regulations and incorporate 'lifetime homes' standards into their construction plans. Registered social landlords (largely housing associations) building homes subsidised with public money through the Housing Corporation are also now required to meet scheme development standards that cover similar areas to 'lifetime homes'. The idea here is that housing should be as healthy and enabling as possible at the point of construction.

One example of the Government's commitment to tackling the unhealthiness of the existing housing stock is the introduction of a new Housing Health and Safety Rating Scheme to replace the Fitness for Human Habitation standard (Housing below Tolerable Standard in Scotland).[11] The new system will assess and grade dwellings in all tenures specifically from a health and safety perspective. The standard is evidence-based and grounded in the findings of the housing and health research effort. This revision is important because the standard will be used by local authorities as the basis for action, as was the previous Fitness standard. Whether a dwelling provides acceptable living accommodation or needs to be improved is now based not simply on its physical condition, but on the risk it poses to occupants' health and safety. This, moreover, is determined by considering both the physical fabric of the home *and* the vulnerability of occupants to its potentially health and safety harming effects.[11]

In order to achieve such standards of healthiness and safety across the private housing stock, the Government plans to overhaul the existing local authority private sector renewal and home improvement system. Local authorities are to be awarded a new general power to give financial and practical assistance (either directly themselves or via organisations such as home improvement agencies) for home improvement, repair and adaptation in order to encourage and/or subsidise home owners to improve their own homes. The new general power will also offer new freedoms to declare renewal areas and group repair schemes, and to waive the repayment of housing renewal grants in certain circumstances.[12] This increased local authority discretion is designed to provide the freedom to offer a wider range of assistance for dealing with poor condition housing.

A key aim of the new approach to home improvement, however, is to increase individual householder funding of repairs, adaptation and maintenance. Notwithstanding the limited increase in public financing of the grant system since 1997 (enabling an increase in maximum grant values and the capital and income eligibility thresholds as well as additional support to help disabled people meet their contributions towards adaptation grants) and the extension of the (separate) Home Energy Efficiency Scheme, which offers insulation and heating improvements to those most at risk from ill health, the new strategy does not amount to a new collective responsibility for healthy private housing. There are no signs of a reversal of the shift in responsibility for housing repair, maintenance and improvement costs from the state to the individual that took place during the two preceding decades.

To address the situation in the social rented sector, the Government has pledged that all social housing in England will be brought up to a 'decent standard' by 2010. This commitment will similarly be supported by some additional public resources (including a new Major Repairs Allowance of £1.6 billion in 2001/02, credit approvals, arm's length arrangements and the use of capital receipts) and also private money through Private Finance Initiative (PFI) schemes.[10]

Not only does this new national healthy housing programme rely on increased private funding, but, as the Government acknowledges, it also depends on the imagination and commitment of a range of local housing (and health) agencies. There is currently evidence to suggest that local authorities and other local housing agencies and providers have taken up this challenge. Indeed, many have been delivering the type of publicly and privately funded healthy housing initiatives alluded to in national policy documents, for many years. In some cases, they have also succeeded in highlighting the public health gains of such housing investment.

A number of particularly innovative schemes based around the idea of 'repairs on prescription' aim to improve the health of asthmatic children by upgrading the heating and draught-proofing of their family homes. Grants or financial assistance are offered to households nominated by general practitioners or other health professionals. These schemes, managed by local authorities, draw on health services funding to repair poor council housing, on the grounds that this will, in the long run, reduce demand on the health services.[13,14] There is some evidence that such housing improvement for health schemes can work,[15,16] though not conclusively so.[17,18]

Local home maintenance initiatives, including a range of schemes to encourage home owners to maintain and improve the conditions of their homes, have also been established throughout the country by local authorities, home improvement agencies and housing associations, sometimes in collaboration with social service authorities.[19,20] They include local advice and information centres, local classes to raise awareness of the need for repair, tool loan or hire schemes, lists of reliable builders, organisation of 'group maintenance' schemes and handypersons' schemes. In particular, pilot handypersons' schemes to provide assistance to home owners with small repairs and minor adaptations have been found to provide a valuable service at the intersection of housing and community care, with beneficial effects for the health, safety and wellbeing of vulnerable groups.[19]

The dramatic improvements to health and quality of life of housing investment in the course of urban regeneration have also been documented. Local programmes to remove and replace poor housing can lead to significantly lower levels of illness and fewer visits to GPs among sick people and those most at risk of ill health,[21,22] though the detrimental health effects of the renewal process itself have also been highlighted.[23]

Because of the complex – and often poorly understood – ways in which housing specifications, quality and conditions interact with health problems (and with a range of other factors affecting health), the quest for healthy housing has so far taken the form of a set of locally limited experiments. However, as more of these experiments are documented and the evidence base for healthy housing interventions grows, policy makers will have fewer grounds for failing to build an explicit health dimension into housing strategies on a much larger scale.

Housing for health

The main objective of any healthy housing policy has to be to maintain a healthy housing environment in every part of the housing stock. Until this objective is met, however, there will always be a need for strategies which protect those whose health is most at risk, and which secure shelter for people on the basis of health need. It is this principle that lies at the core of the long-established practice of awarding priority to people with health problems in the queue to move into, or within, the stock of state-subsidised rented housing.

Medical priority for rehousing

Although moving house has been identified as a stressful life event that can precipitate both mental and physical illness, medical priority rehousing (MPR) is a form of residential mobility that is explicitly designed to be therapeutic. It is based on the idea that if the existing home has detrimental effects on occupants' health – by causing or increasing susceptibility to disease, exacerbating illness or disability, or impeding access to care – then moving home may help to cure sickness, alleviate suffering, improve ability to cope with ill health and/or enhance access to care. In short, medical priority for rehousing aims to work as a health intervention by moving sick and disabled people to homes more suited to their health needs. It is thus a practical means of making the most effective use, in health terms, of the existing housing stock. Notwithstanding the fact that this practice has so far been confined to the social rented sector, MPR represents the most important housing programme helping sick people to move out of, or avoid moving into, unhealthy homes. Currently, virtually all local authorities and most housing associations in Britain award some priority in their housing queues to people with health and mobility problems.[24,25]

The assessment of health needs and the award of medical priority for rehousing often involves public health physicians, GPs, occupational therapists and/or other health professionals.[26,27] However, MPR is primarily a housing initiative. Despite little statutory guidance, housing managers have worked for more than 50 years on the assumption that health status is a valid criterion for the allocation of state-subsidised rented housing. Indeed, it is notable that medical needs have come to occupy a prominent position among the range of housing needs that are routinely recognised as attracting priority status in the British social housing sector. Health needs can carry enough weight in housing allocations to ensure rehousing outcomes that are favourable in terms of housing and neighbourhood quality, and health and quality of life.[25,28]

The problem is that this particular healthy (re)housing solution is one that is in short supply. Medical priority systems are under increasing pressure in many parts of the country. The most important challenge comes from the privatisation of the social housing system, in particular the decline in both the size and quality of the local authority housing stock over the past 20 years.[24] This places systems under strain, struggling to cope with increasing demand from people with health problems. Consequently, only a small proportion of those in need of medical priority rehousing will be rehoused.

A further challenge to the idea of medical rehousing for health might come from the changed *character* of a restructured social housing system. Housing policy over the past 20 or so years has not only hinged on reducing the size of the social housing stock, but is about encouraging its distribution among a wider range of not-for-profit landlords – landlords who may have less experience of, and commitment to, the idea of housing for health. In particular, local authorities have been encouraged to transfer their housing stock to other social housing organisations, including housing associations and local housing companies. Housing associations are now seen as the main providers of new social rented housing. Yet we know that the tradition of rehousing sick and disabled people is not so widespread nor so firmly entrenched in the housing association sector as the council sector.[24]

This means there is an increasingly limited capacity – and, possibly, commitment – to accommodate growing demand from people with health and mobility needs.[29] The idea of social housing for health is more open to question now than at any time in the past 50 years. This therefore raises important questions about how sick and disabled people, including those who could previously have relied on MPR, fare in the market sector of the housing system.

Healthy housing markets?

The housing market consists of a number of forms of tenure, but by far the biggest part of this sector – and the largest housing tenure overall – is owner occupation. This, moreover, is the part of the housing system that has grown most rapidly in recent years, largely at the expense of local authority renting. It is also the housing tenure that has been promoted, by the previous Conservative and current Labour administrations alike, as the norm to which all households should aspire.[10,30]

As housing opportunities in the social sector have declined, people with health problems have increasingly been forced to turn to the housing market to accommodate their housing needs. But there are also a number of reasons why this group might *choose* to become or remain home owners; reasons why they, like the rest of the population, might aspire to owner occupation.

The attractions of owner occupation are numerous and include choice and control regarding where, and in what type of housing, you live; a tax-free investment and store of wealth; the prospect of cheap housing services in old age; a sense of ontological security; and a position within the healthier segment of the national housing stock.[31,32] Of course, sick people are just as likely to want these benefits as well people, but crucially they might be in greater *need* of them. It could be argued that these are benefits that are consistent with the idea of housing for health. Indeed, there is some evidence to suggest that owner occupation may have some direct health- and quality-of-life-promoting effects.[33]

The problem for the nation's health is that the housing market, like all markets, responds to ability to pay rather than to need. Indeed, if anything, this tendency has become more pronounced in recent years. A recent study shows that the housing market does not routinely supply the kinds of homes some people with health problems need at affordable prices.[31] Moreover, the system is rarely geared to helping them find the few suitable properties that do exist.[32] Whereas anyone can find pointers to homes with 'original features', 'mature garden' or 'impeccable décor', few clues exist for buyers about access, mobility standards, adaptations or other health-relevant features. Even when suitable housing can be found, there is still the question of affordability. Low, intermittent, benefit-based incomes are not attractive to mortgage lenders and yet these are just the kind of income experiences that many people with health problems have.[34]

In other words, it could be argued that the principles and practices of the housing market work, generally inadvertently, to the disadvantage of people with health problems. In contrast to the healthy housing tradition of the social sector, it discriminates against, rather than in favour of, health needs. Ironically, this means that the therapeutic qualities of home ownership might be least available to those who need them the most.

This situation arises because the housing market currently has no 'caring' role – or responsibility – to compare with that of the social housing sector. It follows that if housing policy is to succeed in expanding the scope of sustainable home ownership, it will be necessary to build some 'caring' (social) dimensions into this sector. We have made some suggestions to this end.[32,35] Despite expressing a clear preference for the role of the market, recent policy statements acknowledge that it might be time to address the issue, if owner occupation is going to be an option for a wider range of people. A key concern now is 'to make the [housing] market work for all' and to develop policies that deliver a fairer market that protects the vulnerable.[10,36]

To this end, a new power of local authorities to offer financial assistance to help existing owner occupiers buy another property where this is a better option than repairing, improving or adapting their own home[37] is potentially a promising first step. Currently, local authorities are permitted to offer loans at commercial rates, or to offer relocation grants to help people whose homes are subject to a compulsory purchase order only. It is unclear what type of financial assistance the Government has in mind for the new initiative but this could include grants, subsidised loans or help with commercial loan repayments. This new local authority role could also, moreover, be usefully, but easily, extended to include practical assistance to sick and disabled people, among others, in the process of looking for a new home.

Conclusion

Britain has a long tradition of using housing interventions to meet public health goals. For almost a century this tradition has been implicit rather than explicit in many areas of housing provision. However, policy makers, practitioners and the general population have all begun to recognise the importance of good housing to good health. This chapter has charted the impact of this mind-shift by describing two key ways in which public health can be safeguarded by housing interventions. It has argued that the move towards promoting 'Our Healthier Nation' and 'Supporting People' can be achieved both by improving the housing stock and ensuring the availability of healthy homes to those who need them most. The success of such strategies depends on political commitment, adequate finance and an imaginative approach locally to the use of housing investment in both the public and private sectors.

References

1 Clapham D, Kemp P and Smith SJ (1990) *Housing and Social Policy*. Macmillan, Basingstoke.

2 Smith SJ (1989) *Housing and Health. A review and research agenda. Discussion Paper 27*. Centre for Housing Research, University of Glasgow.

3 Department of the Environment, Transport and the Regions (1996) *English House Conditions Survey*. The Stationery Office, London.

4 Scottish Homes (1997) *Scottish House Condition Survey 1996: main report*. Scottish Homes, Edinburgh.

5 Secretary of State for Health (1992) *The Health of the Nation. A strategy for health in England*. Cm 1986. HMSO, London.

6 Secretary of State for Health (1999) *Saving Lives: our healthier nation*. Cm 4386. The Stationery Office, London.

7 Department of the Environment, Transport and the Regions (2001) *Supporting People. Policy into practice.* DETR, London.

8 Secretary of State for Health (1998) *Modernising Social Services.* Cm 4169. The Stationery Office, London.

9 Department of the Environment, Transport and the Regions (1998) *Housing and Regeneration Policy. A statement by the Deputy Prime Minister and Secretary of State for the Environment.* DETR, London.

10 Department of the Environment, Transport and the Regions (2000) *Quality and Choice: a decent home for all.* DETR, London.

11 Department of the Environment, Transport and the Regions (2001) *Health and Safety in Housing. Replacement of the Housing Fitness Standard by the Housing Health and Safety Rating System.* DETR, London.

12 Department of the Environment, Transport and the Regions (2001) *Private Sector Housing Renewal. Reform of the Housing Grants, Construction and Regeneration Act 1996, Local Government and Housing Act 1989 and Housing Act 1985. A consultation paper.* DETR, London.

13 Chartered Institute of Housing (1998) *Housing and Health. Good Practice Briefing 13.* Chartered Institute of Housing, Coventry.

14 Easterlow D (2000) *Poor Housing and Public Health. Developing a strategy for action.* Royal Institute of Public Health and Hygiene and Society of Public Health, London.

15 MacKenzie I (1998) *Housing and Asthma.* Paper presented to the Royal Institute of Public Health and Hygiene with Care & Repair England, 'Poor Housing and Public Health' Conference, London.

16 Inman K (1999) Breath of fresh air. *Guardian Society,* 6 October.

17 Hopton J and Hunt S (1996) The health impacts of improvements to housing: a longitudinal study. *Housing Studies.* 11:271–87.

18 Department of the Environment (1998) *Housing and Health Research: measuring the health benefits of housing improvements.* DoE, Social Research Division, London.

19 Joseph Rowntree Foundation (1996) The value of handyperson's schemes for older people. *Findings in Housing Research,* p179. Joseph Rowntree Foundation, York.

20 Joseph Rowntree Foundation (1999) Local maintenance initiatives for home-owners. *Findings in Housing Research*, p459. Joseph Rowntree Foundation, York.

21 Ellaway A, Fairley A and Macintyre S (1999) *Housing Investment and Health Improvement in Inverclyde*. A report commissioned by the Inverclyde Regeneration Partnership. Social and Public Health Sciences Unit, University of Glasgow.

22 Ambrose P (2000) *A Drop in the Ocean*. Health and Social Policy Research Centre, University of Brighton.

23 Allen T (2000) Housing renewal – doesn't it make you sick? *Housing Studies*. 15:443–61.

24 Smith SJ and Mallinson S (1997) Housing for health in a post-welfare state. *Housing Studies*. 12:173–200.

25 Mason S and Britain A (1998) *Housing Allocations and Medical Priority in Scotland*. The Scottish Office Central Research Unit, Edinburgh.

26 Smith SJ, McGuckin A and Walker C (1994) Healthy alliance? The relevance of health professionals to housing management. *Public Health*. 108:175–83.

27 Easterlow D and Smith SJ (1997) Fit for the future? A role for health professionals in housing management. *Public Health*. 111:171–8.

28 Smith SJ, Alexander A and Easterlow D (1997) Miracle or mirage? *Health and Place*. 3:203–16.

29 Easterlow D (1998) *Housing and Health: a geography of welfare restructuring*. Unpublished thesis, University of Edinburgh.

30 Department of Environment (1995) *Our Future Homes. Opportunity, choice, responsibility*. HMSO, London.

31 Easterlow D, Smith SJ and Mallinson S (2000) Housing for health: the role of owner occupation. *Housing Studies*. 15:367–86.

32 Smith SJ, Easterlow D and Munro M (2001) *Housing as a health intervention: can the market care?* Paper presented to the Annual Conference of the Institute of British Geographers, Plymouth.

33 Macintyre S, Ellaway A, Der G *et al*. (1998) Do housing tenure and car access predict health simply because they are markers of income or self esteem? A Scottish study. *J Epidemiol Community Health*. 52:657–64.

34 Easterlow D, Smith SJ, Munro M and Turner KM (2000) *Health histories and housing careers*. Paper presented to the BSA Annual Conference, 'Making Time/Marking Time', York.

35 Smith SJ, Easterlow D, Munro M and Turner K (2003) Housing as health capital. *J Soc Issues*. (In press.)

36 Armstrong H (1998) Speech by Hilary Armstrong to the Annual Conference of the Chartered Institute of Housing, Harrogate.

37 Department of the Environment, Transport and the Regions (2000) *Quality and Choice: a decent home for all. The way forward for housing*. DETR, London.

Chapter 2

Housing conditions and health consequences

Jane Hopton, Stephen Platt and Linda Macleod

Introduction

Evidence that poor housing contributes to, or causes, poor health has accumulated slowly and in a piecemeal fashion. Over the past 150 years interest has shifted from concerns about overcrowding and sanitation to recognition of the potentially harmful impact of the indoor physical environment and exploration of the consequences of building design for social health and wellbeing. Recent recognition of the problems of homelessness and living in temporary accommodation has brought this research full circle.[1,2]

In theory, there are several different ways to segment the research on housing and health: according to different aspects of housing, according to different health effects, or according to the different groups of people affected. In practice, research has clustered around certain aspects of housing, such as dampness, and specific health effects, such as respiratory illness. This review is structured to reflect these clusters, with subsections on dampness, cold and mental health, although research exploring a range of housing issues, such as noise, overcrowding and security, is also briefly considered.

The chapter begins with an overview of the different ways of conceptualising the relationship between housing and health, the main research approaches and associated methodological issues.

Research approaches and methodological issues

Research on housing and health can be grouped into three approaches: area-based (ecological) studies, studies of the internal environment and studies of housing in social context. Underpinning these approaches are three conceptualisations of the ways in which housing can impact on health (*see* Box 2.1).

Box 2.1: Different conceptualisations of the relationship between housing and health

1   There are the direct physical effects of environmental conditions (e.g. cold) or of pathogens related to poor conditions (e.g. house-dust mites are more prevalent in damp housing and clearly associated with poor respiratory health).
2   There are direct consequences for the inhabitants' family and social life, which in turn are a source of stress and strain, which can cause mental health problems and increase susceptibility to physical illness.
3   There are the indirect health consequences arising from living in poor housing conditions whereby the latter impact negatively on resources and capacity to engage in activities which may promote health or reduce the impact of illness.

Area-based (ecological) studies

Area-based (ecological) studies have demonstrated that people living in areas where housing is poor have poorer health than their counterparts living in areas where housing conditions are better.[3–5] Such studies have been criticised for failing to define what constitutes poor housing and, related to this, for not considering the mechanisms or explanations underpinning these associations.[6,7]

Studies of the internal environment

A contrasting research approach has been to examine the health impact of specific aspects of housing conditions. The focus has been on pollutants or pathogens, which have been shown to have a direct physical impact in experimental or occupational settings. Cold indoor temperatures can also be included as a characteristic of the environment that has direct physical effects. Within this research approach the underlying mechanisms by which housing can contribute to ill health and specific health effects can, in theory, be made explicit.

A range of indoor pollutants or pathogens has been investigated, including:

- the products of fuel combustion for heating or cooking, particularly nitrogen dioxide from the combustion of gas[8–12]
- radon, which occurs naturally in the environment and can accumulate in indoor environments[13–15]
- formaldehyde and other volatile organic compounds released from building materials and furnishings[16,17]
- house-dust mite allergens and fungal mould, both of which are fostered in damp housing.[2,18]

Establishing the relationship between these factors and health can be problematic, since it is necessary to specify which aspects of housing conditions contribute to the proliferation of the pathogen. The housing environment is most usefully conceptualised as a system in which key aspects of housing are inter-related and, as a consequence, different pathogens or factors may co-occur. For example, aspects of housing design which reduce air exchange between the internal and external environment may lead to an increase in relative humidity (dampness) and an increase in exposure to pollutants from cooking and heating.

An understanding of the relationship between housing conditions and health also involves establishing the basic elements of an epidemiological enquiry,[19] namely, the levels of exposure and extent of exposure over time, ruling out confounding factors which may explain an association between housing conditions and ill health, and establishing plausible mechanisms or processes which would explain any associations. Given the scope for generating and testing specific hypotheses about the health effects of these pathogens and for measuring them objectively, this research approach has the potential to produce strong scientific evidence. However, as described below, there are problems with such a narrow understanding of strength of evidence.

Aside from the issue of what constitutes strong scientific evidence, in practical and policy terms there is the issue of establishing the prevalence of these aspects of housing in order to estimate their likely public health impact. For example, while the harmful effects of radon and formaldehyde (or other volatile organic compounds) have been established, the occurrence and levels of these pathogens within the housing stock is not known.[18]

Housing in social context

A third research approach has been to understand the relationship between housing and health in a wider social context, regarding housing as a social and economic environment which influences social activities and daily life, thereby impacting upon health. This type of research has considered issues of housing design, including individual housing units as well as the wider built environment. Research on overcrowding can also be seen to fall within this approach. More recently, the economic impact of poor housing has highlighted the health issue of fuel poverty.

Poor quality housing is more likely to be inhabited by those living on lower income, rather than higher income earners, while damp houses tend also to be colder than dry housing. Work on the energy efficiency of housing has drawn attention to the fact that people with low incomes are more likely to live in the least energy-efficient housing, that is, housing which costs more to heat. A greater proportion of lower incomes is spent on energy and this may still not be sufficient to alleviate the problems of cold and dampness. Within this approach, poor housing is seen to compound the problems of living on a low income rather than low income being seen as a potential confounding factor in the relationship between housing and health. Fuel poverty is likely to impact on resources for healthy eating, socialising and other behaviours which can promote health or prevent illness.

Damp and cold housing

The rationale for including a major section on the health impact of damp and cold housing in this chapter is threefold. First, as many policy and scientific reviews have noted, the prevalence and severity of damp and cold housing within the UK constitutes a significant public health concern that demands to be addressed.[1,2,20] Second, a substantial body of knowledge has accumulated in relation to these aspects of housing. Third, this body of research illustrates well the main methodological issues and the research approaches outlined above, as well as the recurring debates about the relationship between housing and health.

Damp housing

Evidence for the detrimental health effects of damp housing comes from two sources: first, research which has sought to investigate the role of damp housing as a factor in the development of specific illnesses or health problems (principally respiratory illnesses such as asthma and forms of atopy); second, research exploring the health effects of damp housing.

Both of these strands of research are underpinned by similar plausible mechanisms for direct health effects of dampness. Much of the research outlined above has been based on, or refers to, two sources of pathogens, which are known to proliferate in damp housing, namely house-dust mites and fungal mould.

House-dust mites

Experiments involving direct inhalation of dust mites have detected significant bronchial reactivity.[21,22] Many studies have shown the importance of mites as a cause of human allergic diseases, rhinitis and bronchial asthma.[23] When considering asthma in children the most common source of allergen is the house-dust mite.[24] One study found that 94% of 11-year-old children in England with more active asthma were allergic to house-dust mites.[25] Moreover, there is evidence that exposure to house-dust mites at an early age and the development of allergies and asthma in later childhood are associated with severity of asthma symptoms and continuation and severity of symptoms into adolescence.[26] Allergens contained in the bodies of dust mites have been implicated in other atopic illnesses such as eczema.[27] It has been noted that viruses that can give rise to infection are more common in damp houses. Experimental research has established that bacteria thrive in moist conditions, though little work has explored this relationship in domestic settings.[12,28]

Mould

Damp conditions are also conducive to the proliferation of mould and fungal spores which can thrive on the organic matter present in the substance of the house and on furnishings. Some genera of fungi produce metabolites which are toxic. The mycotoxins are contained in the spores and may be inhaled or ingested. Direct physiological responses to mycotoxins produced by fungi which are present in domestic dwellings have been demonstrated in experimental conditions.[29,30] Studies indicate that mould may be responsible for respiratory conditions which are associated with allergenic responses, such as asthma and rhinitis.[31,32] As well as evidence of changes in lung function associated with chronic exposure, there is also evidence of acute symptomatic effects, such as fever and wheezing and other influenza-like symptoms.[33]

Research on damp housing

Case control studies from around the world have explored the role of damp housing in the aetiology of asthma and atopy, principally by seeking to establish higher rates of sensitisation and exposure to house-dust mites and hence higher rates and greater severity of symptoms. Nine studies,[34–42] seven of which were based on children under 16 years of age,[34–36,38–40,42] found that cases with asthma or symptoms of asthma were significantly more likely to be living in damp housing, after controlling for possible confounding factors. Two studies have shown dose response relationships to severity of mould as rated by a surveyor[39] and to increased prevalence of house-dust mite.[37]

Several studies investigated the effects of dampness upon health, although not all of these have sought to explore specific mechanisms for any observed effects by measuring levels of pathogens in the indoor environment. These studies are summarised in Table 2.1. Studies in the Netherlands,[43–45] Sweden,[46] Canada,[47,48] Taiwan,[49] China,[50] Turkey,[51] the United States,[44,53] the United Kingdom[54–56] and Australia[57] have consistently shown that children living in damp houses experience more respiratory symptoms and problems, including cough, wheeze, and nasal congestion and excretion, than children in dry homes, independently of potential confounding factors. A recent longitudinal study in the UK showed that respiratory symptoms of children diagnosed as having asthma reduced significantly after installation of central heating.[58]

Most studies have relied on parental reports of symptoms using validated questionnaires, together with self-report or interviewer assessments of problems of dampness and mould. It has been suggested that self-reports of dampness may be unreliable or subject to reporting bias.[59] Some studies, which have used objective measures of health status, have failed to find significant associations. However, these objective measures of respiratory health are known to be unreliable and their relevance in terms of respiratory function in everyday circumstances is questionable.[59] For example, overall measures of airborne fungal mould spores which do not distinguish between different genera of fungi have been criticised, as not all fungi have toxic effects. Where reported measures of dampness have been compared with objective measures, self-reports tend to underestimate the levels of dampness.[55] The most robust evidence comes from a study in which measurements of fungal spore counts were taken by surveyors who were blind to the findings of a health survey.[55] The study showed a dose response relationship, with children living in

continued on page 32

Table 2.1: Epidemiological studies of housing conditions and health

Study	Study population	Design	Measure of housing	Measures of health	Confounding factors	Findings
Brunekreef et al.[52]	4625 8–12-year-old school children from six US cities.	Cross-sectional survey – self completion questionnaire.	Reported dampness problems of water collecting in the basement floor, any water damage to the building, mould or mildew on any surface in the home or dampness (any of the above).	American Thoracic Division Lung Disease Respiratory Symptom Questionnaire. Other non-chest illness restricting the child's activities for three days or more in the past year. Height, weight and measure of lung function FEV1.	Presence or absence of mother who smokes in the home, mean number of years parents in education, city of residence, doctor diagnosed asthma.	Significant association between measures of home dampness and respiratory symptoms and non-chest illness after adjusting for confounding factors.
Brunekreef[44]	Two populations of 6–12-year-old schoolchildren in the Netherlands. Survey 1: 1051 children. Survey 2: 3344 children.	Two cross-sectional surveys – self-completion questionnaire.	Reported presence of damp stains and visible mould growth in past two years.	Survey 1 included spirometry tests. Both included reported symptoms of cough, wheeze and asthma or any of the above. Cough on most days for at least three months consecutively. Wheeze or whistle sounds in the last year. Attacks of shortness of breath with wheezing in the last year.	Children smoking. Household smoking. Sources of nitrogen dioxide (measured in Study 1). Parental education.	Reported respiratory symptoms significantly associated with damp stains and mould after controlling for other variables. No clear association with lung function.

Author	Sample	Study design	Exposure measure	Outcome measure	Confounders	Results
Brunekreef[45]	3344 adult parents of children aged 6–12 years (see Brunekreef et al.[44]).	Cross-sectional survey using self-completion questionnaire.	Dampness in home: presence of damp stains or visible mould growth within the past two years. Presence of gas-fired water heaters.	Respiratory symptoms, chronic bronchitis (cough and phlegm) and asthma (wheeze, attacks of shortness of breath). Reported allergy for pollen or house-dust.	Parental educational level, smoking habits.	Cough and phlegm and any lower respiratory symptoms were significantly associated with home dampness after controlling for active and passive smoking, indoor nitrogen dioxide sources and education level. The association for asthma and allergy were not significant when confounders taken into account.
Dales et al.[47]	14 948 school children aged 5–8 years in 30 different communities in Canada.	Cross-sectional survey using self-completion questionnaire.	Reported number of mould sites, wet or damp spots appearing in past year, flooding in the past year and dampness (any of the above).	American Thoracic Society Division of Lung Disease Respiratory Symptom Questionnaire. Plus non-respiratory symptoms, e.g. headaches, muscle aches, fever, chills, nausea, vomiting or diarrhoea, eye irritations on three or more separate occasions in the last three months.	Age, sex, race, highest level of education, number of household smokers, cooking fuel, heating (gas or kerosene), hobbies, sex of respondent and region of residence, physician confirmed allergy to mould.	Prevalences of all respiratory symptoms were higher in homes with reported moulds or dampness. Adjusted and unadjusted odds ratios were similar.

Study	Study population	Design	Measure of housing	Measures of health	Confounding factors	Findings
Dales et al.[48]	14 799 adults over 18 in 30 different communities in Canada.	As above.	As above.	American Thoracic Division Lung Disease Respiratory Symptom Questionnaire.	As above.	Prevalence of cough, phlegm, wheeze higher amongst those reporting dampness or mould independently of confounding factors.
Garret et al.[57]	148 children aged 7–14 living in 80 households in Latrobe Valley, Australia.	Cross-sectional survey.	Measures of housing: air samples (total and viable fungal spore levels and genera), temperature and humidity. Reported age and foundation type of residence, presence of air conditioning and dampness. Interviewer assessment of evidence of water intrusion, visible mould and odour.	Respiratory questionnaire: frequency of eight respiratory symptoms: cough, shortness of breath, waking due to shortness of breath, wheeze, asthma attack, chest tightness, cough in morning, chest tightness in morning. Skin prick tests for atopy.	Parental allergy, smoking, parental asthma, presence of pets.	Asthma, atopy and respiratory symptoms were all significantly associated with exposure to one or more genera of fungal spores. Average or total fungal spore counts not significantly associated with health outcomes.
Hopton and Hunt[7]	254 households, 251 children on a single local authority housing estate in Glasgow, UK.	Longitudinal survey quasi-experimental design comparing households where new heating system installed versus 'controls'.	Reported problems with dampness, mould, cold, poor repair, noise, security and cost of heating.	Reported symptoms checklist of 15 respiratory and non-respiratory symptoms in past two weeks.	Household income. Presence of young children. Financial difficulties. Smoking. Unemployment.	No significant effects of introduction of new heating scheme on symptoms. Overall symptoms score significantly associated with deterioration in housing (house becoming too cold).

Study	Sample	Study design	Housing measures	Health measures	Confounders	Results
Hyndman[71]	60 Bengali households in inner-city London, UK.	Cross-sectional interview survey.	Reported housing type, leisure, heating, ventilation, working facilities, reported damp, cold and mould, and aspects of health relating to respiratory and other conditions. Weekly average and spot measures of temperature and humidity. Reported cold, fungal spore counts.	Reported wheezing, breathlessness, coughing, blocked up nose. Three or more above constituting 'hidden asthma', chesty colds, bronchitis or asthma, aches and pains, headaches, diarrhoea and vomiting. Lung function (peak flow).	Smoking. Social class. Occupations.	No significant reduction in peak flow for those in damp, mouldy or cold housing. Significantly higher levels of hidden asthma, chest ill health associated with low indoor temperatures (0–16 degrees). No significant differences in reported and objective health measures and temperatures, humidity and fungal spore counts.
Li et al.[50]	1340 primary school 8–12-year-old children in Taipei, China.	Cross-sectional self-completed questionnaire survey.	Reported home considered damp by residents, visible mould, stuffy odour, water damage, flooding and dampness as assessed by presence of any mould, odour, water damage or flooding.	Cough present for at least three months of the year, phlegm present for at least three months of the year, wheezing in chest on most days or nights, exercise-induced cough, chest illness requiring child to stay at home for at least three days, physician diagnosed asthma and allergic rhinitis.	Age, sex, parents' education, number of household smokers, use of gas stove for food preparation.	Prevalence of all respiratory symptoms higher in damp homes (any aspects of dampness), with significant differences adjusted for confounding factors or phlegm, allergic rhinitis and bronchitis.

Study	Study population	Design	Measure of housing	Measures of health	Confounding factors	Findings
Martin et al.[54]	358 households in Edinburgh, UK.	Cross-sectional blind survey of housing and health.	Independent measures of damp, presence of fungal mould – dampness regarded as any of above signs of damp. Respondent reported dampness.	Reported checklist of symptoms present in past two months – 8 non-respiratory and 4 respiratory. Adults completed a standardised measure of perceived health status – the Nottingham Health Profile.	Smoking and presence of other children in the household, length of time at address, household income, use of calor gas for heating.	Adults: only scores on emotional reaction scale of the Nottingham Health Profile (NHP) were significantly higher in damp houses. Children: presence of any respiratory symptoms, aches and pains, nerves and headaches significantly higher in damp houses. Main effect for respiratory symptoms remained after controlling for confounding factors. Rates of vomiting and sore throat significantly higher in 'mouldy' houses.
Packer et al.[58]	5347 residents in Worcester, England.	Cross-sectional postal questionnaire survey.	Reported heavy condensation, damp or mould (never or hardly ever, not very often, quite often, almost always). Damp housing classified as damp or mould quite often or almost always, condensation almost always.	General household survey question on long-standing illness – checklist of specific illnesses. The Nottingham Health Profile (NHP).	Smoking, exercise, weight, alcohol, social class and housing tenure.	People in damp housing more likely to report long-standing illness – this could not be explained by presence of specific medical conditions. Also more likely to report problems with sleep, energy and social isolation dimensions of NHP.

Study	Sample and design	Measures	Health outcomes	Confounders	Results
Platt et al.[55]	597 households with at least one child (adult respondents and 1169 children) in three UK cities (Glasgow, Edinburgh and London). Cross-sectional survey with independent assessments of housing conditions (by surveyor) and health (by researcher).	Measures of dampness: severity and type. Mould: severity and location. Air samples from rooms where visible mould growth (spore concentration per m² air).	Children's list of 16 symptoms in past two weeks. Adults' checklist of 17 symptoms. Score on General Health Questionnaire (30-item version).	Household income, cigarette smoking, unemployment, overcrowding.	Adults more likely to report more symptoms overall, including nausea and vomiting, blocked nose, breathlessness, backache, fainting and bad nerves than in damp houses. Children in damp and mouldy houses had greater respiratory symptoms, wheeze, sore throat, runny nose, headaches and fever. Mean number of symptoms showed close response relationship with severity of dampness and mould.
Ross et al.[70]	297 children aged 54–59 months in one general practice population in UK. Cross-sectional survey with independent assessments of housing conditions and health.	Temperature and humidity recording over six days during the six-month study period.	Consultations for upper respiratory tract infections or recording of episode of one or more of cold, coryza, cough, sore throat, tonsillitis, pharyngitis, acute otitis media, over the past two weeks.		No association between upper respiratory tract infection and domestic temperatures or humidity.

Study	Study population	Design	Measure of housing	Measures of health	Confounding factors	Findings
Somerville et al.[58]	72 children with diagnosed asthma living in 59 damp houses in Cornwall.	Longitudinal survey (three months follow-up) after installation of heating.	Assessments of type of heating, presence of dampness, mould and insulation. Home energy efficiency rating.	Reported asthma, respiratory symptoms questionnaire covering frequency during previous month of breathlessness, breathlessness on exercise, wheezing (day and night), diarrhoea and nasal symptoms.	Furry pets. Smoking. Type of house.	All respiratory symptoms significantly reduce after intervention.
Spengler et al.[53]	12 842 9–11-year-old children in 24 North American communities.	Cross-sectional self-completed questionnaire survey.	Inventory of home appliances, fuel types used, air conditioning, presence of moisture, water damage or moulds, pets and age of residence. Home dampness defined as presence of moisture, water damage or mould.	Symptoms of asthma: persistent wheeze, attacks of shortness of breath with wheeze, physician diagnosis of asthma. Symptoms of bronchitis: chronic cough, chronic phlegm bronchitis in the past year. Lower respiratory symptoms: wheeze, cough, phlegm, bronchiolitis. Hay fever or allergies, parental asthma or parental chronic obstructive pulmonary disease (COPD).	Gender, parental asthma, parental COPD and parental education.	Composite variable home dampness, and individual variables of presence of mould and presence of water damage all significantly associated with increased symptoms of asthma, bronchitis and lower respiratory symptoms when controlling for confounding factors.

| Strachan and Elton[56] | 165 children aged 7–8 years registered with one general practice in Edinburgh, UK. | Cross-sectional postal survey. | Reported crowding, child's bedroom unheated, windows left open in child's bedroom, presence of unvented gas appliance, coal appliance, dampness (yes/no) mould (yes/no). | Reported respiratory symptoms, coughing during the night and days lost from school because of chest problems in the last school term. Reported attacks of wheezing, fever in the past two years. Medical record entries – not respiratory problems. | Family history of wheeze, family size, other children, parental smoking. | Reports of wheeze, nocturnal cough and school absence for chest trouble were significantly more common among children from damp, mouldy housing. There was no similar consistent relationship in relation to general practice consultations. |
| Strachan and Sanders[68] | 1000 (778 for measures of housing) primary school children age 6.5–7.5 years in Edinburgh, UK. | Cross-sectional survey postal questionnaire, measurements in the home and clinical tests on children. | Reported housing problems including heating and ventilation in child's bedroom, condensation on windows, condensation or damp on the walls, visible mould growth, relative humidity of child's bedroom during the week of the survey, bedroom temperature. | Reported respiratory symptoms in the past year. FEV1 before and after exercise. | Non-reported as paper concentrates on objective measures of housing and respiration for which there were no significant univariate associations. | A significantly greater proportion of children in damp homes were affected by wheeze, day cough, night cough and chesty colds. Measures of relative humidity and temperature showed no associations with respiratory symptoms and no correlations found between bedroom conditions and measured ventilatory function. |

houses with the highest prevalence of airborne mould spores having significantly more respiratory symptoms when confounding factors had been taken into account.

Although most of the studies focused on respiratory health, some asked about general health. Martin et al.[54] found that children living in damp housing were more likely to have experienced aches and pains, nerves and headaches, and that those living in houses with mould were more likely to have experienced vomiting and sore throat. In the study by Platt et al.,[55] dampness was associated with reports of sore throat, headaches and fever, and with the mean total number of symptoms, while Waegemaekers et al.[43] found that dampness was related to headache, tiredness, earache, skin irritation and nausea.

Few studies have explored the health impact on adults. Three studies have found associations between dampness and respiratory symptoms[43,45,48] (see Table 2.1). Platt et al.[55] found higher rates of nausea, vomiting, blocked nose, breathlessness, fainting and bad nerves amongst adults living in damp houses. In a study by Packer et al.,[60] reported dampness was associated with higher rates of long-standing illness, problems with sleep, energy and social isolation, as measured by the Nottingham Health Profile.[61] There is further evidence that dampness has a detrimental effect on mental health, as below.

As indicated above, much of the evidence for the effect of house-dust mite falls into the strand of research which seeks to explain occurrence of specific illness or symptoms and has used case-control designs. The role of house-dust mite in more general non-specific symptoms and health problems remains plausible but less clear. None of the studies exploring the health effects of dampness has attempted to isolate the contribution of house-dust mites to associations found between levels of dampness and health. However, a case-control study found a significant effect of dampness on respiratory symptoms over and above the effect of levels of house-dust mite.[42]

Health implications of cold housing

Few studies have directly examined the relationship between cold housing and health, and evidence for the likely impact derives from two sources: first, observation of seasonal trends in mortality and morbidity and international comparisons of housing conditions derived from national surveys of climate and excess winter deaths[62–64] and, second, experimental and observational research on the direct physiological effects of exposure to cold which may be implicated in both respiratory problems and heart disease.

Much of the work has focused on the impact on the elderly, since this is a group which experiences physiological disadvantage in relation to exposure to cold and also has a more sedentary lifestyle, being likely to spend more time at home.[65–67]

Excess winter deaths

Several analyses have used excess winter deaths at a national level and aggregate indicators of climate and housing conditions to explore the health effect of poor housing.[62–64,68] Excess winter deaths are often due to myocardial infarction, strokes and respiratory conditions. In an early example of this approach, Boardman[62] suggested that 30–60 000 excess deaths in winter would not have occurred in countries with colder climates and warmer homes. However, later analyses have suggested that it is changes in temperature rather than low average temperatures that lead to the excess,[69] although improved housing conditions would mitigate against the effects. In this context, the UK climate can be seen as harsh rather than moderate, with frequent changes in climatic conditions that in turn have detrimental effects on housing conditions.

With the exception of investigations of hypothermia in the elderly, there have been no systematic studies of the impact of cold housing on health status. However, there is both epidemiological and experimental evidence to indicate a relationship between exposure to cold and physiological changes that may be implicated in both respiratory disorders and in heart disease.

Exposure to severe cold gives rise to increased pulmonary flow resistance and decreased forced expiratory volume in sensitive people. Cold air can act as a trigger of bronchospasm[70] and has been linked with impaired lung function in men as measured by forced expiratory volume.[71] These findings were independent of smoking. A rapid change in temperature produces greater respiratory effects than a gradual one (e.g. moving between warm and cold rooms).

A strong association between wheezing in children and cool bedrooms has been reported by Ross et al.[72] Hyndman[73] showed that reported and measured low temperatures were associated with poor chest health.

Two important risk factors for heart disease, hypertension and elevated fibrinogen levels, are associated with low temperatures. Entering a cold room can cause transient hypertension.[74] Blood pressure in normotensive people and people with untreated hypertension has been shown to increase in winter months.[66]

It has been suggested that the cardiovascular changes which perpetuate hypertension may result from acute surges of blood pressure rather than from sustained high levels. Thus repeated exposure to cold could be a factor in the development of essential hypertension.

The risk of ischaemic heart disease is related to plasma fibrinogen levels and the general viscosity of the blood. Cold increases blood viscosity and fibrinogen has been found to be significantly and negatively related to environmental temperature.[75]

Collins[67] has suggested that four dwelling temperature zones are significant for human health. Below 6°C there is risk of failing thermoregulation and hypothermia. Below 12°C there is risk of increased cardiovascular strain and below 16°C risk of respiratory disease. A temperature of 18°C to 24°C is required for comfort. In addition, constant discomfort and the social consequences of cold housing may give rise to significant emotional distress.

Mental health and housing

Most of the research on the mental health impact of housing has considered the impact of housing on social relationships or activities which thereby affect mental health. Research in this area is under-pinned by three themes: the impact of rehousing,[54,76,77] crowding in the dwelling[78] and architectural design.[79-82]

Research into the impact of rehousing to better quality accommo-dation has found conflicting findings in terms of the overall changes in health status, including mental health. Studies have drawn atten-tion to the importance of taking account of the disruption to social networks caused by rehousing, a factor which could explain the absence of a positive effect of rehousing on mental health despite the amelioration of problems caused by poor quality housing.[6,54,76,83]

Crowding is known to be associated with the spread of infectious diseases, and the improvements in population health following public health housing developments in the late nineteenth and early twenti-eth century are attributed in part to reductions in deaths from infectious diseases (*see* Chapter 1). More recent studies of crowding within dwellings have used both objective measures of crowding, based on the number of rooms and number of inhabitants, as well as perceptions of crowding.[6] Both have been shown to be associated with emotional distress. Crowding within dwellings enforces social contact and the continual presence of others has been shown to impose a mental strain on both children and adults and can impair social relationships and activities. Children's play, for example, can be constrained by lack of space.[84]

There has been less research on the mental health impact of differ-ent aspects of poor housing. Two ecological studies comparing people living in housing that was difficult to let with people in better areas found that the former experienced poorer emotional wellbeing. Men in poor housing areas were three times as likely, and women twice as likely, to have symptoms of emotional distress compared to people in better housing areas.[3,4]

Studies which have considered specific aspects of poor housing have investigated the mental health impact of noise, security, damp-ness and poor repair, or combinations of these factors. Noise has been shown to have deleterious psychological effects,[85,86] particularly when it is unpredictable, intermittent and uncontrollable, such as that emanating from noisy neighbours or traffic. The effects of noise have been demonstrated by poor performance on cognitive tests, increased irritability, poor concentration and slower reaction times.[87] Despite good reason to expect that noise can be a significant contributor to emotional distress and poor mental health, there have been no epidemiological studies of noise disturbance in domestic settings.

There is substantial evidence of associations between damp housing and poor mental health. The seminal work by Brown and Harris[88] identified housing dampness as a factor in their analysis of the social origins of depression. Several of the studies of the health effects of damp housing have collected and analysed data on reported emotional symptoms together with standardised measures of mental health. Hyndman[73] reported a strong association between both objective and subjective measures of dampness and reported depression. Martin et al.[54] found that adults living in damp houses had significantly higher scores on the emotional reaction scale of the Nottingham Health Profile.

The General Health Questionnaire (GHQ)[89] has been extensively used as an indicator of the risk of mental illness, principally anxiety and depression. Two studies,[90,91] using the standard cut-off of five or more to indicate 'possible psychiatric caseness' on the 30-item version of the GHQ, found that respondents living in damp houses were significantly more likely to score in excess of the threshold, independently of confounding factors such as social class, employment status, household income, presence of long-standing illness and other housing problems. Although the threshold of five or more is lower than that recommended for detecting clinically relevant mental health problems amongst general practice attenders, both studies found that over 50% of respondents living in damp houses had high GHQ scores, suggesting that the level of associated distress is substantial.[92]

Although the studies by Platt et al.[90] and Hopton and Hunt[91] were mainly concerned with the effects of damp and cold, they also collected data on a range of reported housing conditions, such as noise, security, crowding, poor repair and bad design. Hunt[93] showed that as the number of reported housing problems increased, so did scores on the GHQ and the likelihood of reporting other symptoms of mental distress, such as bad nerves or feeling low and irritable.

Conclusions

The evidence base

Although the evidence base is considerable, and the existence of a strong association between housing and health has been amply demonstrated, few studies have employed a research design that permits robust conclusions to be drawn about causal pathways and processes.[94] There are major methodological difficulties in disentangling different aspects of poor housing and distinguishing the effects of housing from other aspects of social-economic disadvantage which are associated with living in poor housing.

Reviewing the evidence from a social policy perspective gives a different interpretation and illustrates the drawbacks of using a narrow scientific interpretation of evidence. Within this perspective the methodological problem of confounding becomes transformed into a central topic of investigation and policy intervention (*see* Chapter 1). Recent recognition of fuel poverty illustrates this conceptual transformation very clearly, taking a more integrated approach to understanding the health disadvantage of poor housing.

Implications for primary care

With the comprehensive policies and strategies now in place to tackle social inequalities in health and promote social inclusion, together with the strengthening of primary care organisations and their health-improving partnerships, there are important opportunities for individual practitioners, primary care teams, primary care groups and primary care trusts to promote health by addressing the problems of poor housing.[95,96]

Individual practitioners and primary care teams can be encouraged to consider the impact of poor housing conditions on health problems in their clinical assessments of patients, helping to identify vulnerable people and families and to encourage or refer them to the schemes and agencies which can reduce expenditure and improve housing by improving energy efficiency. Schemes are now in place across the UK to ensure that all people living in social housing or aged over 60 have working central heating. Many local authorities and their partners are developing local fuel poverty strategies.[97] Primary care teams can consider routinely collecting information on housing conditions for both planning and research purposes.[98,99]

Primary care groups and primary care trusts can advocate for health in the development of local housing plans and policies through community planning and community care planning processes, ensuring that housing-related health problems and fuel poverty feature in their own plans.

References

1 Acheson D (1991) Health and housing – annual lecture. *J R Soc Health.* **December:** 236–43.
2 Hunt SM (1997) Housing-related disorders. In: J Charlton and M Murphy (eds) *The Health of Adult Britain 1841–1994.* Vol. 1, pp156–70. The Stationery Office, London.
3 Blackman T, Evason E, Melaugh M and Woods R (1989) Housing and health: a case study of two areas of Belfast. *J S Policy.* **18:**1–26.
4 Keithley J, Byrne D, Harrison S and McCarthy P (1984) Health and housing conditions in public sector housing estates. *Public Health.* **98:**344–53.
5 Brennan M and Lancashire R (1978) Association of childhood mortality with housing status and unemployment. *J Epidemiol Community Health.* **32:**28–33.
6 Kasl SV (1974) Effects of housing on mental and physical health. *Man Environment Systems.* **4:**207–26.
7 Hopton J and Hunt SM (1996) The health effects of improvements to housing: a longitudinal study. *Housing Studies.* **11:**271–86.
8 Melia RJW, Chinn S and Rona RJ (1990) Indoor levels of NO_2 associated with gas cookers and kerosene heaters in inner-city areas of England. *Atmospheric Environment, Part B-Urban*

Atmosphere **24**:177–80.

9 Melia RJ, Florey CD, Chinn S *et al.* (1985) Investigations into the relations between respiratory illness in children, gas cooking and nitrogen dioxide in the UK. *Tokai J Exp Clin Med.* **10**:375–8.

10 Melia RJ, Florey CD, Morris RW *et al.* (1982) Childhood respiratory illness and the home environment. 1. Relations between nitrogen dioxide, temperature and relative humidity. *Int J Epidemiol.* **11**:155–63.

11 Pilotto LS and Douglas RM (1992) Indoor nitrogen dioxide and childhood respiratory illness. *Aust J Public Health.* **16**:45–250.

12 Samet JM, Marbury MC and Spengler JD (1987) Health effects and sources of indoor air pollution. Part I. *Am Rev Respir Dis.* **136**:1486–508.

13 Rannou A (1990) Radon in dwellings: physical and health properties. *Endeavour.* **14**:34–9.

14 Bowie C and Bowie SH (1991) Radon and health. *Lancet.* **337**:409–13.

15 Stuart BO (1989) Radon exposure estimates. *Toxicol Lett.* **49**:341–8.

16 Broder I, Corey P, Brasher P *et al.* (1988) Comparison of health of occupants and characteristics of houses among control homes and homes insulated with urea formaldehyde foam. III. Health and house variables following remedial work. *Environ Res.* **45**:179–203.

17 Broder I, Corey P, Brasher P *et al.* (1991) Formaldehyde exposure and health status in households. *Environ Health Perspect.* **95**:101–4.

18 Samet JM, Marbury MC and Spengler JD (1988) Health effects and sources of indoor air pollution. Part II. *Am Rev Respir Dis.* **137**:221–42.

19 Bradford Hill A (1965) The environment and disease: association of causation? *Pro R Soc Med.* **58**:295–300.

20 Best R (1999) Health inequalities: the place of housing. In: D Gordon, M Shaw, D Dorling and G Davey Smith (eds) *Inequalities in Health: the evidence.* Policy Press, Bristol.

21 M'Raihi L, Charpin D, Thibaudon M and Vervloet D (1990)

Bronchial challenge to house dust can induce immediate bron-choconstriction in allergic asthmatic patients. *Ann Allergy.* 65:485–8.

22 Ostergaard PA, Ebbesen F, Nolte H and Skov PS (1990) Basophil histamine release in the diagnosis of house-dust mite and dander allergy of asthmatic children. Comparison between prick test, RAST, basophil histamine release and bronchial provocation. *Allergy.* 45:231–5.

23 Korsgaard J and Iversen M (1991) Epidemiology of house dust mite allergy. *Allergy.* 46 Suppl. 11:14–18.

24 Duff AL and Platts-Mills TA (1992) Allergens and asthma. *Pediatr Clin North Am.* 39:1277–91.

25 Sporik R, Chapman MD and Platts-Mills TA (1992) House dust mite exposure as a cause of asthma. *Clin Exp Allergy.* 22:897–906.

26 Nicolai T, Illi S and von Mutius E (1998) Effect of dampness at home in childhood on bronchial hyperreactivity in adolescence. *Thorax.* 53:1035–40.

27 Carswell F and Thompson SJ (1987) Percutaneous sensitisation to house-dust mite may occur naturally in eczema. *Int Arch Allergy and Appl Immunol.* 82:453–5.

28 Arundel AV, Sterling EM, Biggin JH and Sterling TD (1986) Indirect health effects of relative humidity in indoor environments. *Environ Health Perspect.* 65:351–61.

29 Smith JE, Anderson JG, Lewis CW and Murad YM (1992) Cytotoxic fungal spores in the indoor atmosphere of the damp domestic environment. *FEMS Microbiol Lett.* 79:337–43.

30 American Academy of Pediatrics Committee on Environmental Health (1998) Toxic effects of indoor moulds. *Pediatrics.* 101:712–14.

31 Hosen H (1978) Moulds in allergy. *J Asthma Res.* 15:151–6.

32 Burr ML, Mullins J, Merrett T and Stott N (1988) Indoor moulds and asthma. *J R Soc Asthma.* 108:99–102.

33 Tobin R, Baranowski E and Gilman A (1987) Significance of fungi in indoor air: report of a working party. *Can J Public Health.* 78:1–14.

34 Dotterud LK, Korsgaard J and Falk ES (1995) House-dust mite content in mattresses in relation to residential characteristics and symptoms in atopic and non-atopic children living in northern Norway. *Allergy.* 50:788–93.

35 Mohamed N, Ng'ang'a L, Odhiambo J *et al.* (1995) Home environment and asthma in Kenyan schoolchildren: a case-control study. *Thorax.* 50:74–8.

36 Nordvall SL, Eriksson M, Rylander E and Schwartz B (1988) Sensitization of children in the Stockholm area to house dust mites. *Acta Paediatr Scandinavica.* 77:716–20.

37 Korsgaard J (1983) Mite asthma and residency. A case-control study on the impact of exposure to house-dust mites in dwellings. *Am Rev Respir Dis.* 128:231–5.

38 Lindfors A, Wickman M, Hedlin G *et al.* (1995) Indoor environmental risk factors in young asthmatics: a case-control study. *Arch Dis Childhood.* 73:408–12.

39 Williamson IJ, Martin CJ, McGill G *et al.* (1997) Damp housing and asthma: a case-control study. *Thorax.* 52:229–34.

40 Yang CY, Tien YC, Hsieh HJ *et al.* (1998) Indoor environmental risk factors and childhood asthma: a case-control study in a subtropical area. *Pediatr Pulmonol.* 26:120–4.

41 Iversen M and Dahl R (1990) Allergy to storage mites in asthmatic patients and its relation to damp housing conditions. *Allergy.* 45:81–5.

42 Nafstad P, Oie L, Mehl R *et al.* (1998) Residential dampness problems and symptoms and signs of bronchial obstruction in young Norwegian children. *Am J Respir Crit Care Med.* 157:410–14.

43 Waegemaekers M, Van Wageningen N, Brunekreef B and Boleij JS (1989) Respiratory symptoms in damp homes. A pilot study. *Allergy.* 44:192–8.

44 Brunekreef B (1992) Associations between questionnaire reports of home dampness and childhood respiratory symptoms. *Sci Total Environ.* 127:79–89.

45 Brunekreef B (1992) Damp housing and adult respiratory symptoms. *Allergy.* 47:498–502.

46 Andrae S, Axelson O, Bjorksten B *et al.* (1988) Symptoms of

bronchial hyperreactivity and asthma in relation to environmental factors. *Arch Dis Childhood.* **63**:473–8.

47 Dales RE, Zwanenburg H, Burnett R and Franklin CA (1991) Respiratory health effects of home dampness and molds among Canadian children. *Am J Epidemiol.* **134**:196–203.

48 Dales RE, Burnett R and Zwanenburg H (1991) Adverse health effects among adults exposed to home dampness and molds. *Am Rev Respir Dis.* **143**:505–9.

49 Yang CY, Chiu JF, Chiu HF and Kao WY (1997) Damp housing conditions and respiratory symptoms in primary school children. *Pediat Pulmonol.* **24**:73–7.

50 Li CS and Hsu LY (1996) Home dampness and childhood respiratory symptoms in a subtropical climate. *Arch Environ Health.* **51**:42–6.

51 Yazicioglu M, Saltik A, Ones U *et al.* (1998) Home environment and asthma in school children from the Edirne region in Turkey. *Allergol Immunopathol.* **26**:5–8.

52 Brunekreef B, Dockery DW, Speizer FE *et al.* (1989) Home dampness and respiratory morbidity in children. *Am Rev Respir Dis.* **140**:1363–7.

53 Spengler J, Neas L, Nakai S *et al.* (1994) Respiratory symptoms and housing characteristics. *Indoor Air.* **4**:72–82.

54 Martin CJ, Platt SD and Hunt SM (1987) Housing conditions and ill health. *BMJ.* **294**:1125–7.

55 Platt S, Martin CJ, Hunt SM and Lewis CW (1989) Damp housing, mould growth, and symptomatic health state. *BMJ.* **298**:1673–8.

56 Strachan DP and Elton RA (1986) Relationship between respiratory morbidity in children and the home environment. *Fam Pract.* **3**:137–42.

57 Garrett MH, Rayment PR, Hooper MA *et al.* (1998) Indoor airborne fungal spores, house dampness and associations with environmental factors and respiratory health in children. *Clin Exp Allergy.* **28**:459–67.

58 Somerville M, Mackenzie I, Owen P and Miles D (2000) Housing and health: does installing heating in their homes improve the

health of children with asthma? *Public Health.* 114:434–9.

59 Strachan DP (1988) Damp housing and childhood asthma: validation of reporting of symptoms. *BMJ.* 297:1223–6.

60 Packer CN, Stewart-Brown S and Fowle SE (1994) Damp housing and adult health: results from a lifestyle study in Worcester, England. *J Epidemiol Com Health.* 48:555–9.

61 Hunt SM, McKenna SP and McEwen J (1980) A quantitative approach to perceived health. *J Epidemiol Comm Health.* 34:281–5.

62 Boardman B (1986) *Seasonal Mortality and Cold Homes. Unhealthy Housing: a diagnosis.* University of Warwick.

63 Isaacs N and Donn M (1993) Health and housing: seasonality in New Zealand mortality. *Aust J Public Health.* 17:68–70.

64 McKee M, Sanderson C, Chenet L *et al.* (1998) Seasonal variation in mortality in Moscow. *J Public Health Med.* 20:268–74.

65 Otty CJ and Roland MO (1987) Hypothermia in the elderly: scope for prevention. *BMJ.* 295:419–20.

66 Woodhouse PR, Khaw KT and Plummer M (1993) Seasonal variation of blood pressure and its relationship to ambient temperature in an elderly population. *J Hypertens.* 11:1267–74.

67 Collins KJ (1986) Low indoor temperatures and morbidity in the elderly. *Age & Ageing.* 15:212–20.

68 Eng H and Mercer JB (1998) Seasonal variations in mortality caused by cardiovascular diseases in Norway and Ireland. *J Cardiovasc Risk.* 5:89–95.

69 Rudge J (1996) British weather: conversation topic or serious health risk? *Int J Biometeorol.* 39:151–5.

70 Strachan DP and Sanders CH (1989) Damp housing and childhood asthma; respiratory effects of indoor air temperature and relative humidity. *J Epidemiol Comm Health.* 43:7–14.

71 Rasmussen F, Borchsenius L, Winslow J and Ostergaard E (1978) Associations between housing conditions, smoking habits and ventilatory function in men with clean jobs. *Scandinavian J Respir Dis.* 59:264–76.

72 Ross A, Collins M and Sanders C (1990) Upper respiratory tract infection in children, domestic temperatures, and humidity. *J Epidemiol Comm Health.* 44:142–6.

73 Hyndman SJ (1990) Housing dampness and health amongst British Bengalis in east London. *Soc Sci Med.* **30**:131–41.

74 Tochihara Y, Ohnaka T, Nagai Y *et al.* (1993) Physiological responses and thermal sensations of the elderly in cold and hot environments. *J Thermal Biol.* **18**:355–61.

75 Keatinge W, Coleshaw S and Cotter F (1984) Increases in platelet and red cell counts, blood viscosity and arterial pressure during mild surface cooling: factors in mortality from coronary and cerebral thrombosis in winter. *BMJ.* **291**:1405–8.

76 Wilner D, Walkley RP, Schram JM *et al.* (1960) Housing as an environment factor in mental health. *Am J Public Health.* **50**:55–63.

77 Elton PJ and Packer JM (1986) A prospective randomised trial of the value of rehousing on the grounds of mental ill-health. *J Chronic Dis.* **39**:221–7.

78 Gabe J and Williams P (1986) Is space bad for your health? The relationship between crowding in the home and emotional distress in women. *Sociol Health Ill.* **8**:351–71.

79 Hannay DR (1981) Mental health and high flats. *J Chronic Dis.* **34**:431–2.

80 Birtchnell J, Masters N and Deahl M (1988) Depression and the physical environment: a study of young married women on a London Housing Estate. *Br J Psych.* **153**:56–64.

81 Moore NC (1974) Psychiatric illness and living in flats. *Br J Psych.* **125**:500–7.

82 Gillis AR (1977) High rise housing and psychological strain. *J Health and Social Behavior.* **18**:418–31.

83 Wilner D, Walkley RP, Pinkerton TC and Tayback M (1969) *The Housing Environment and Family Life.* The Johns Hopkins Press, Baltimore.

84 Hartup W (2001) Children and their friends. In: D Carson (ed.) *Man-Environment Interactions: evaluation and applications.* Environmental Design Research Association, Milwaukee.

85 Gloag D (1980) Noise and health: private and public responsibility. *BMJ.* **281**:404–7.

86 Lowry S (1990) Families and flats. *BMJ.* **300**:245–7.

87 Bastenier H, Klosterkoetter W and Large J (1975) *Environ Quality of Life: damage and annoyance caused by noise*. EUR 5398e, Commission of the European Communities, Brussels.

88 Brown GW and Harris TO (1978) *The Social Origins of Depression: study of psychiatric disorder in women*. Tavistock Publications, London.

89 Goldberg DP (1972) *The Detection of Psychiatric Illness by Questionnaire*. Oxford University Press, London.

90 Platt S, Martin CJ and Hunt S (1990) The mental health of women with children living in deprived areas of Great Britain: the role of adverse living conditions, poverty and unemployment. In: D Goldberg and D Tantam (eds) *The Public Health Impact of Mental Disorder*, pp124–35. Hogrefe and Huber, Gottingen.

91 Hopton J and Hunt SM (1996) Housing conditions and mental health in a disadvantaged area in Scotland. *J Epidemiol Com Health*. **50**:56–61.

92 Wright AF and Perini A (2001) Hidden psychiatric illness: use of the general health questionnaire in general practice. *J R Coll Gen Pract*. **37**:164–7.

93 Hunt SM (1990) Emotional distress and bad housing. *Health & Hygiene*. **11**:72–9.

94 Thomson H, Pettigrew M and Morrison D (2001) Health effects of housing improvement: systematic review of intervention studies. *BMJ*. **323**:187–90.

95 Department of the Environment (2001) *UK Fuel Poverty Strategy*. DoE, London.

96 Olsen NDL (2001) Prescribing warmer, healthier homes. *BMJ*. **322**:749–50.

97 City of Edinburgh Council (2001) *An Affordable Warmth Strategy for Edinburgh*. City of Edinburgh Council, Edinburgh.

98 Smeeth L and Heath I (1999) Tackling health inequalities in primary care [editorial]. *BMJ*. **318**:1020–1.

99 Hopton J, Howie JGR and Porter AMD (1991) Social indicators of health needs for general practice: a simpler approach. *B J Gen Pract*. **42**:236–40.

Chapter 3

Homelessness and health: the role of primary care

Helen Lester

The Royal College of General Practitioners has stated that all people must have equity of access to primary care services.[1] This chapter will look at various aspects of homelessness, concentrating on specific health issues and the current and potential future role of primary care in delivering equitable and accessible services to homeless people.

Defining homelessness

Homelessness is an ambiguous term that has no universally accepted definition. The current legal definition in the 1996 Housing Act is shown in Box 3.1.

This statutory definition, however, excludes major groups of homeless people such as the single homeless and couples without children. The current legislation also excludes asylum seekers from statutory help unless they applied for asylum at the port of entry to the UK or if there has been an 'upheaval' declaration in their country of origin.

The definition of homelessness widely accepted by many non-statutory organisations is *a lack of decent, safe and secure housing*, acknowledging the fluid boundaries at which poor physical conditions in a dwelling effectively make the occupants homeless.[2] Others

Box 3.1: The legal definition of homelessness in the United Kingdom (UK)

A person is deemed as homeless and owed a duty of housing if they fulfil the following criteria:

- have no accommodation in the UK or elsewhere in the world
- cannot secure entry to accommodation
- are threatened with homelessness in the next 28 days and have no accommodation which it is reasonable for them to occupy
- are not intentionally homeless
- have a local connection with the area
- are in priority need – *pregnant/with dependent children/ vulnerable due to old age or mental illness or physical disability/homeless due to fire, flood or other disaster.*

have spoken of homeless careers, acknowledging that it is impossible to capture the characteristics of all homeless people within a single definition of homelessness[3] or suggest that homelessness is typified by a lack of a stable support network such as family and friends.[4] The Royal College of General Practitioners has stressed that homelessness extends beyond the familiar images of people sleeping rough under bridges, to encompass hostel dwellers, travellers, families in bed and breakfast (B&B) accommodation, people in squats and those in temporary or overcrowded accommodation.[1]

Measuring homelessness

The lack of a common practical definition of homelessness creates significant problems with measuring the real extent of housing need and therefore in planning appropriate health and social service responses.

In 2000, 172 760 households were officially recognised as homeless by local authorities in England, representing approximately 415 000 people.[5] There are, however, no comprehensive national statistics available for unofficial homeless people, that is people who are homeless but fall outside the legal definition of homelessness and eligibility. There are, however, an estimated 17 700 people living in hostels in England outside London and approximately 14 700 in hostels in London.[6] Information on the number of people sleeping rough is the most difficult to obtain. Department of Environment figures in 1997 estimated that there were 1095 people sleeping rough in the UK. Shelter, however, estimates that there are up to 2500 people sleeping rough in the UK.[7] Hidden homelessness, that is the number of potential homeless households, which includes overcrowded households, is also a significant problem in the UK. A survey of English housing conducted by the Office for National Statistics showed that 478 000 households were living in statutorily overcrowded conditions.[8]

Causes of homelessness

The underlying causes of homelessness are complex and multiple and can only be briefly signposted in this chapter. Structural explanations look beyond the individual and consider broader social and economic causes such as housing and welfare policy as causes of homelessness. Most analyses of the causes of homelessness in the UK have focused on the mismatch between the level of housing need and the supply and accessibility of housing in the public, private rented and home ownership sector.[9] There have, for example, been three key and mutually reinforcing factors within national housing policy since 1979 which have particularly contributed to this mismatch: the sharp reduction in public sector building, the 'Right to Buy' policy which encouraged people to buy their rented council houses leading to both a depletion and residualisation of stock, and the switch in finance from new building to other forms of incentive and support. In contrast, the agency explanations of homelessness divide into two strands. In the first, individuals are seen as responsible and to blame for their own homelessness. They are, in essence, part of the historical 'undeserving' poor. This argument is often associated with the stereotype of the homeless middle-aged alcoholic or teenage substance abuser and with pregnant teenage girls.[10] The second strand of the agency argument maintains that people become homeless because of personal failure or inadequacy for which they cannot be held entirely responsible, such as adverse childhood experiences. They are in effect the 1990's equivalent of the Victorian 'deserving' poor. There is some evidence, despite the probable existence of confounding variables, that childhood abuse,[11] childhood adversity such as poor parenting with lack of affection,[12] and being brought up in local authority care are risk factors for future homelessness.[13] It is postulated that being brought up in an institution may lead to domestic de-skilling with inadequate preparation for independent living and a lack of adequate support systems.[14] However, arguments that emphasise the particular individual characteristics of homeless people are in danger of reinforcing stereotypes about homeless people and diverting attention from the macro causes of homelessness such as welfare and housing policy.

Describing homelessness

Anyone can become homeless. It has been shown that up to 4.3% of the current heads of households in England have experienced a period of homelessness in the past decade.[15]

Demographic details of the official/ statutorily homeless population

The most recent examination of the demographic details of the official homeless population was provided by the *Survey of English*

Housing 1994/5[16] based on interviews with 20 000 heads of house-holds in England. Secondary analysis of data provided demographic details about people who had approached a local authority in relation to their perceived homelessness and who had been accepted as offi-cially homeless.[15] The analysis showed a clear association between age and homelessness, with 1196 (14%) young people between 16 and 29 years and 2961 (6%) of those between 30 and 44 years stating that they felt themselves to have been homeless in the past ten years. After the age of 45, the chances of experiencing homelessness declined markedly. The experience of homelessness was also found to be great-est amongst heads of households who identified themselves as black, with a black head of household over three times more likely to have experienced homelessness than a white head of household. This may be because of discrimination in housing allocation. However, more recent evidence suggests that it is not ethnicity *per se*, but a combina-tion of other factors such as living in an urban area and low rates of economic activity, more common in black and minority ethnic groups, that increase the chances of homelessness.[15]

Demographic details of the unofficial/ non-statutorily homeless population

The most recent comprehensive survey of unofficially homeless people was conducted by the Centre for Housing Policy.[6] This study included interviews with 1346 single homeless people in hostels and bed and breakfast accommodation and also 507 users of day centres and soup runs who were sleeping rough. Of the hostel population, 969 (77%) were male, and 456 (91%) of the rough sleepers were male. However, compared with earlier surveys[17] these figures suggest that there has been an increase in the proportion of homeless women in hostels over the last 20 years. People from black or other minority ethnic groups were over-represented in the hostel and B&B accommodation and under-represented among the rough sleepers.

Of the people sleeping rough, 492 (97%) described themselves as White UK as did 921 (73%) of the single homeless people in B&B accommodation.

During the last decade there has also been an increase in the unofficial young homeless population. Shelter estimates that over 246 000 young people experience homelessness annually.[8] Young people are excluded from accommodation under the homelessness legislation unless they are deemed vulnerable. Youth homelessness is growing due to changes in the welfare system which make it difficult for young people to find and then maintain temporary or permanent housing. People aged 16 and 17 years old are not entitled to income support and 18–25-year-olds received a lower level of housing benefit and income support, making homelessness more likely. Young people leaving care face particular hardship. They are expected to become independent at an earlier age than other young people and often experience a lack of support. A study found that over half the 16- and 17-year-olds and 39% of the 18–24-year-olds living in temporary accommodation had lived in care, hospital or another type of institution at some point.[6]

Homelessness and health

There is a substantial body of evidence linking homelessness with poor health.[9] It is, however, notoriously difficult to disentangle the cause and effect of homelessness and health. Morbidity may also be linked with age, sex, ethnicity, employment, personal behaviour such as smoking, and genetic variation, as well as the variation caused by the type of homelessness, subsequent accommodation and the length of homelessness. The following general statements can, however, be made with some authority, namely that health problems may predate homelessness, homelessness may cause health problems to appear, homelessness may cause existing health problems to become worse and health problems may also be a cause of homelessness.[9]

Homelessness as a cause of poor health

Homelessness represents an increased risk to health because it means that individuals are exposed to a range of factors that are associated with poor health. There is an increased risk of contracting infectious diseases because of overcrowded, cold, damp, unsanitary conditions.[18] The incidence of tuberculosis (TB) among homeless people was also significantly greater than among the housed population. In 1994, Crisis found a prevalence of 2% among the 611 single homeless people screened for TB in London.[19] Problems associated with poverty, such as poor diet and inadequate heating, and the use of coping strategies such as smoking and drinking, also increase risks to health. There is also an increased risk of trauma because of the risk of violence faced by rough sleepers in particular[20] and an increased risk of accidents among homeless children in temporary accommodation.[21] Several of these risks are not unique to homeless people. Many housed people on low incomes are also subject to similar risks to health, such as poor diet and stress. However, homelessness lies at the extreme of the housing continuum, and as the environment in which someone is homeless becomes more unfit for habitation, health risks increase.[6]

Homelessness as an exacerbating factor of poor health

Homelessness can also prolong or exacerbate poor health. Existing illness can be compounded by all the factors mentioned previously and also by poor access to medical care. Compliance with advice and treatment is also difficult when there is nowhere to rest and keep warm and when general diet and nutrition are poor, in an environment where medication may be stolen, where it is difficult to keep to strict times for taking tablets and where there is no reliable address for sending further appointments.

Poor health as a cause of homelessness

Evidence is increasingly emerging that people with health problems are falling out of the housing system and becoming homeless.[22] People experiencing intermittent or permanent health problems are, for example, more likely to experience difficulties securing a sufficiently large and stable income to pay a deposit for accommodation or repay a mortgage. Ill health can also increase the risk of unemployment, subsequent mortgage or rent arrears and therefore of homelessness.[9]

People with mental health problems may also face an additional increased risk of homelessness because of discrimination in terms of job opportunities and because the socio-economic forces that cause homelessness, such as high unemployment, seem to affect the most vulnerable groups in society disproportionately.[22] Evidence on the prevalence of mental health problems in the homeless population provided by a joint initiative between the Mental Health Foundation and the Department of Health found that 31% of homeless people had a possible psychosis compared to 0.5–1% of the housed population, 2% had a drink problem, 2% were involved in drug misuse and 10% had some other form of mental illness.[23] The more recent OPCS survey across the UK found even higher rates of alcohol dependence, of 16% of hostel residents, 44% of night shelter residents and 50% of day centre visitors.[24]

The extent of drug abuse among the single homeless population is not clear, partially because of the methodological flaws in previous surveys, and partially because it is difficult to make categorical statements about a sensitive issue such as drug use when replies may imply a criminal usage. There appear to be two broad patterns of abuse: abuse of prescribed medication and abuse of non-prescribed or street drugs. Bines reported rates of dependency on street drugs of 3% among hostel and B&B dwellers, 7% among rough sleepers using day centres and 9% among those using soup runs.[25] OPCS data once again found higher rates of dependency on non-cannaboid drugs, of 6% of hostel residents, 13% of those using day centres and 22% of those living in night shelters. The same survey found the use of any drug varied from 25% among hostel dwellers, 37% for day centre users and 46% for night shelter residents.[24] Flemen found that homeless young people were twice as likely to take cannabis than non-homeless young people, and eight times more likely to take heroin. This increased to 18 times more likely for those sleeping rough.[26]

The medical priority system for housing allocation is also unreliable in practice and open to abuse by those best placed to mobilise the system to their own advantage.[27] Allocation procedures are therefore not always consistently selective in favour of those with health problems. The poor health profile of homeless people therefore stems, in part, from the fact that those with health problems can become excluded from the housing system.

Standardised morbidity rates (SMRs) of homeless people

A survey of the self-reported health of single homeless people living in hostels and B&B accommodation and rough sleepers using day centres and soup runs exemplifies many of the health problems associated with homelessness.[25] Compared to the general population, single homeless people were more likely to have health problems and more likely to have more than one health problem. People sleeping rough experienced the worst health of all (*see* Table 3.1).

Mortality of rough sleepers

A study by Crisis, using the London Coroner's Courts, found that 74 deaths of rough sleepers had been recorded and that life expectancy was 42 years, compared with the national average of 74 years for men and 79 years for women.[20] Crisis also found that rough sleepers were 35 times more likely to kill themselves than the general population and four times more likely to die from unnatural causes such as accidents, assaults, murder, drug or alcohol poisoning.

Table 3.1: Standardised morbidity rates (SMRs) of reported health problems of single homeless people[25]

Health problem	Hostel and B&B SMR	Day centre SMR	Soup runs SMR
Musculoskeletal problems	153	185	221
Difficulty in seeing	166	313	308
Difficulty in hearing	148	163	166
Skin complaints/wound infections	105	189	298
Chronic chest/breathing problems	183	259	365
Heart problems	54	64	66
Digestive problems	183	244	265
Depression/anxiety	785	1072	1152
Fits/loss of consciousness	651	2109	1892

Primary care for homeless people

Homeless people are less likely to be registered with a general practitioner (GP) than the housed population. Registration rates for homeless people varies between 24% and 92%, the former described in a study of rough sleepers[28] and the latter in families in B&B accommodation.[29] The recent report from the Centre for Housing Policy in York[30] found that 46% of homelessness projects for single homeless people and rough sleepers across England reported that permanent registration with a GP was generally available, 40% that temporary registration was available and 14% that registration was not generally available. This in turn means that homeless people are less likely to receive health promotion advice and health prevention services such as screening and immunisation. They are also less likely to be able to build up a relationship with a GP and to receive the continuity of care that is potentially important in disease detection and health education. Patients also rely on the GP's gatekeeping role in terms of accessing prescriptions, providing referral on to secondary care services and co-ordinating follow up.

There have been a number of studies attempting to understand the reasons behind these lower registration rates. Previous work from the viewpoint of the GP suggests that the major barriers to primary health care are a combination of practice and system disincentives focused around perceived demand in terms of time and financial cost,[31] poor support from allied services such as social services[32–34] and a lack of relevant training.[2,34,35] GPs have also been described as reluctant to provide care because of fears that homeless people would be excessively mobile, abusive and disruptive.[31,35–39] The potentially negative reaction of other patients has also been mentioned as a barrier.[31,34,35,37] The barriers created directly by the GP are also alluded to in terms of the feelings engendered in providing care for homeless people.[40]

Studies investigating the reality of accessing primary healthcare from the viewpoint of homeless people show that they appear to be acting rationally in making a decision not to seek help early in the course of an illness because they expect and accept that illness is inevitable in their situation and the cost–benefit ratio is not in favour of seeking care.[41] If they do decide to seek primary care, the major barriers appear to be the negative reactions of the receptionists and the GPs[20,21,41–44] and the problems created by a healthcare system that relies on a permanent address.[20,33,34,39,42,45] Added to this is a sense of powerlessness and stigmatisation.[32] The reluctance of homeless people to use primary care services, even if they do register, coupled with the GPs' reluctance to accept them, may result in what has been described as a 'cycle of reluctance'.[46]

Current service provision

In order to plan appropriate primary care services for homeless people in the twenty-first century, the accessibility, environment, coverage and quality of care of models of provision and the evidence provided by previous research on barriers to primary care need to be taken into account (*see* Box 3.2). There is a greater degree of urgency around this issue at the moment since the impact of the Home Office Dispersal Scheme for asylum seekers has meant greater involvement

of GPs with little previous experience of meeting the needs of homeless people.

Box 3.2: Criteria for evaluation of primary care services

Access
* Availability when required.
* Effect on responsibility perceived by other providers.

Quality of care
* Range of services.
* Standard of services.
* Health prevention as well as immediate treatment.

Environment
* Contribution to segregation.

Coverage
* Suitable for all people's needs.

Separate/specialised services

In the last 15 years there have been a number of initiatives in the
provision of separate services, including the use of salaried GPs,[47] the
appointment of house doctors[48] and setting up mobile surgeries.[45,49]
Proponents of this method suggest that homeless people prefer separate services.[50] In 1996, a report for the Department of Health (DoH)
noted that there were 13 dedicated primary care homelessness centres
in England.[51]

Personal Medical Services (PMS) pilot schemes have led to a
dramatic increase in the number of dedicated primary care homelessness centres. In guidance from the DoH, prior to the call for
applications for first-wave PMS schemes, homeless people were
specifically mentioned as a target group for PMS projects.[52] There are

currently 25 primary care centres around the country under PMS contracts and specialising (or with a special interest) in the healthcare of homeless people. There are also several other specialist homelessness centres around the country that have contractual arrangements other than PMS.

It is important, however, that specialised homelessness centres working under a PMS contract are not seen as a panacea for all homeless people. Their obvious strength is that they overcome the time–cost disincentive to GPs working with homeless people. PMS contracts have the potential to replace or complement the capitation system of payment which forms a significant proportion of GP independent contractor pay. The obvious limitations of specialised services are that they may effectively absolve local GPs from providing primary care services and at worst may serve to ghettoise homeless people rather than encouraging integration back into mainstream primary care.

Integrated services

At the other end of the spectrum from separate services are fully integrated services, where homeless people would be expected to access and use mainstream general practice. Mainstream services offer advantages in terms of enabling access to a wide range of ordinary primary care-based services, including those for women's health, in a non-segregated environment and also increase the availability of out-of-hours cover. However, the potential problems of mainstream provision for homeless people include the lack of flexibility of services, such as the predominance of booked surgeries rather than immediate access 'walk in' surgeries. The methods of funding in primary care may also not be sufficiently flexible at present to take into account the potential extra workload that homeless people can represent in terms of morbidity. The impact of registering a significant number of homeless families on target payments for cervical smears and immunisations also needs to be resolved. Deprivation payments that may help to offset the additional workload would be difficult to calculate since homeless people can be difficult to define and enumerate. There are also potential problems caused by mainstream general practice's ability to network efficiently with other statutory and voluntary homeless service providers and potential for perceived negative reactions from reception staff, housed patients and from the GPs themselves, some of whom may be conscripts rather than converts.

The future?

PMS is unlikely to be the sole solution in tackling health inequalities of homelessness. Perhaps a better model would be a seamless service provision between specialised and mainstream primary care services. This would involve homeless people, for example rough sleepers, registering with a specialised homeless practice when they are in crisis. Once their urgent needs have been met by the specialist skills available in such services they could then be helped to permanently register within mainstream general practice. This model creates a bridge between separation and integration, opening up access to mainstream care for the majority of homeless people and also providing immediate transitional primary healthcare and social care services through interested GPs.

In 1993, the DoH endorsed a model of specialist provision of primary care for homeless people through the funding of 35 specialist projects.[53] The three-year evaluation of these projects, however, emphasised that they were generally more successful in providing good quality specialist care than achieving integration back into mainstream primary care. The funding, networking, support and training issues for mainstream services therefore need to be addressed if this model is to work effectively.

Primary care trusts (PCTs), with their dual remit to work more closely with social services departments (and indeed to have the potential for unified budgets for health and social care) and to commission primary healthcare for large populations, could be pivotal in organising and supporting this service model. Central policy developments around extending the nurse role in primary care also have potential to significantly improve the health of homeless populations. Nurse practitioners working alongside general practitioners in their practices could play a central role in supporting mainstream primary care, ensuring smooth transition of homeless people from specialised primary care centre to mainstream general practice, signposting to resources, and enabling effective networking with housing and social care. Registration policies and health prevention payments may also require increased flexibility and imagination from PCTs and strategic health authorities, and training may be required for practice staff to dispel barrier-inducing stereotypes of homeless people.

Conclusion

Homelessness can affect anyone and has a direct effect on health. There is therefore a need for accessible, appropriate, good quality primary care services for homeless people. Current evidence, however, would suggest that this is not always the case. Significant changes are needed to maximise the health and welfare outcomes for homeless people and bring primary healthcare for homeless people into the twenty-first century. Such changes require debate and discussion between planners, providers and homeless people to ensure services are appropriate and acceptable.

The limited evidence on the different models of service provision suggest that specialist services are perhaps best suited to respond to the immediate needs of homeless people, followed by supported integration back into mainstream primary care. Recent changes in health and social sector organisation offer new opportunities to develop innovative service models.[54,55]

In conclusion, whilst it would be wrong to castigate primary care as a major cause of the health problems of homeless people, it is perhaps time for primary care teams, PCTs, social services and strategic health authorities to reflect on the current provision of services for this group of people, and to consider how, together, we can work towards equity of access to primary care services.

References

1 Royal College of General Practitioners (1993) *Statement on Homelessness and Primary Care.* RCGP, London.
2 Access to Health (1993) *Good Practice in General Practice.* Access to Health, London.
3 Moore J, Canter D, Stockley D and Drake M (1995) *The Faces of Homelessness in London.* Dartmouth Publishing, Aldershot.
4 Lamb H (1984) *The Homeless Mentally Ill.* American Psychiatric Association, Washington DC.
5 Kincaid S (2000) *A New Approach to Homelessness and Allocation.* Shelter Publications, London.
6 Anderson I, Kemp PA and Quilgars D (1993) *Single Homeless People.* HMSO, London.
7 Shelter (1998) *Behind Closed Doors: the real extent of homelessness and housing need.* Shelter Publications, London.
8 Diaz R and Coleman B (1997) *Who Says There's No Housing Problem? Facts and figures on housing and homelessness.* Shelter Publications, London.
9 Connelly J and Crown J (1994) *Homelessness and Ill Health: Report of a Working Party of the Royal College of Physicians.* Royal College of Physicians, London.
10 Lowe S (1997) Housing tenure. In: J Goodwin and C Grant (eds) *Built to Last? Reflections on British Housing Policy.* Roof, London.
11 Boule I (1993) Youth homelessness and health care. In: K Fisher and J Collins (eds) *Homelessness, Health Care and Welfare Provision.* Routledge, London.
12 Craig T *et al.* (1990) *The Homeless Mentally Ill Initiative: an evaluation of four clinical teams.* Department of Health and Mental Health Foundation, London.
13 Lupton C (1985) *Moving Out: older teenagers leaving residential care.* Social Services Research and Intelligence Unit, Portsmouth.
14 Kemp P (1997) The characteristics of single homeless people in England. In: R Burrows, N Pleace and D Quilgars (eds) *Homelessness and Social Policy.* Routledge, London.

15 Burrows R (1997) The social distribution of the experience of homelessness. In: R Burrows, N Pleace and D Quilgars (eds) *Homelessness and Social Policy*. Routledge, London.

16 Green H, Thomas M, Iles N and Down D (1996) *Housing in England 1994/5: a report of the 1994/5 Survey of English Housing*. HMSO, London.

17 Digby PW (1976) *Hostels and Lodgings for Single People*. HMSO, London.

18 Barry U (1992) Young homeless people: key issues. In: P Aggleton and I Warwick (eds) *Young People, Homelessness and HIV/AIDS*. Health Education Authority, London.

19 Shanks NJ, George SL, Westlake L and Al-Kalai D (1994) Who are the homeless? *Public Health*. **108**:11–19.

20 Crisis (1996) *Still Dying for a Home*. Crisis, London.

21 Standing Conference on Public Health (1994) *Housing, Homelessness and Health*. Nuffield Provincial Hospitals Trust, Oxford.

22 Vincent J (1995) *Homeless Single Men – roads to resettlement?* Avebury, Aldershot.

23 Craig TK and Hodson S (1998) Homeless youth in London: childhood antecedents and psychiatric disorder. *Psychol Med*. **28**:1379–88.

24 Gill B (1996) *OPCS Surveys of Psychiatric Morbidity in Great Britain. Report 7. Psychiatric morbidity among homeless people*. HMSO, London.

25 Bines W (1994) *The Health of Single Homeless People*. University Centre for Housing Policy, University of York.

26 Flemen K (1996) *Smoke and Whispers. Drug and Youth Homelessness in Central London*. The Hungerford Drug Project, London.

27 Robinson D (1998) Health selection in the housing system: access to council housing for homeless people with health problems. *Housing Studies*. **13**:23–4.

28 Leddington S (1989) Sometimes it makes you frightened to go to hospital . . . they treat you like dirt. *Health Serv J*. **11**:21–2.

29 Victor CR (1992) Health status of the temporarily homeless

population and residents of North West Thames region. *BMJ.* **305**:387–90.

30 Pleace N, Jones A and England J (2000) *Access to General Practice for People Sleeping Rough.* Centre for Housing Policy, York Publishing Services Ltd.

31 Wood N, Wilkinson C and Kumar A (1997) Do the homeless get a fair deal from general practitioners? *J R Soc Health.* **117**:292–7.

32 Stern R, Stilwell B and Heuston J (1989) *From the Margins to the Mainstream: collaboration in planning services with single homeless people.* West Lambeth Health Authority, London.

33 Hinton T (1994) *Battling Through the Barriers.* Health Action for Homeless People, London.

34 Pleace N and Quilgars D (1996) *Health and Homelessness in London.* King's Fund, London.

35 Williams S and Allen I (1989) *Health Care for Single Homeless People.* Policy Studies Institute, London.

36 Leighton J (1976) Primary medical care for the homeless and rootless in Liverpool. *The Hospital and Health Services Review.* **72**:266–7.

37 Manchester Central Community Health Council (1980) *Health Care for Homeless People.* CHC, Manchester.

38 Bone M (1984) *Registration with General Medical Practitioners in Inner London: a survey carried out on behalf of the DHSS.* HMSO, London.

39 Bayliss E and Logan P (1987) *Primary Health Care for Homeless Single People in London. A strategic approach.* SHIL, London.

40 Holden HM (1975) Medical care of homeless and rootless people. *BMJ.* **4**:446–8.

41 Shiner M (1995) Adding insult to injury: homelessness and health service use. *Soc Health Ill.* **17**:525–49.

42 Hinton T (1992) *Health and Homelessness in Hackney.* Medical Campaign Project, London.

43 Holland AC (1996) The mental health of single homeless people in Northampton hostels. *Public Health.* **110**:299–303.

44 Lester HE and Bradley CP (2001) Barriers to primary health care for homeless people – the general practitioner perspective. *European J Gen Pract.* **7**:6–12.

45 Ramsden SS, Nyiri P, Bridgewater J and El-Kabir DJ (1989) A mobile surgery for the single homeless people in London. *BMJ.* **298**:372–4.

46 Fisher K and Collins J (eds) (1993) *Homelessness, Health Care and Welfare Provision.* Routledge, London.

47 Golding AMB (1987) The health needs of homeless families. *J R Coll General Pract.* **37**:433–4.

48 Powell PV (1988) Primary health care for the single homeless. *BMJ.* **297**:84–5.

49 Conway J (1988) *Prescription for Poor Health – the crisis for homeless families.* London Food Commission, The Maternity Alliance, SHAC and Shelter, London.

50 Hewett NC (1999) How to provide for the primary health care needs of homeless people: what do homeless people in Leicester think? *Br J Gen Pract.* **49**:819.

51 Hewett N (1998) *Primary Health Care for Homeless People: a report for the Department of Health.* Department of Health, London.

52 Department of Health (1997) *Personal Medical Services: pilots under the NHS (Primary Care) Act 1997. A comprehensive guide.* HMSO, London.

53 Department of Health (1995) *Review of Primary Care Projects for the Homeless.* Department of Health, London.

54 www.doh.gov.uk/shiftingthebalance/index.htm

55 *Health and Social Care Act, 2001.* The Stationery Office, London.

Chapter 4

Ethnic minority health and housing

Mark RD Johnson and Richard Tomlins

Introduction

For a long time, UK social policy has been 'colour blind' – that is, policy makers and many practitioners have sought to insist that they 'treat all clients equally' and 'take no account of race, ethnicity or skin colour'. This may lead to growing ethnic or 'racial' disparity of treatment and outcome. As ethnic differences in cultural and clinical needs exist, identical treatment that ignores these differences increases rather than decreases inequality of outcome.[1] The 2000 Race Relations Amendment Act[2] places a legal duty on all public services, including housing, to combat discrimination.

Number and settlement pattern

In 1991, the national census showed that 5.5% of the population in Great Britain was of black and minority ethnic (BME) groups.[3] This represented 4.5% of all households, since BME households are slightly larger than white households on average. By 1998, the BME proportion is estimated to have risen to about 7.3% (1 in 14) of the total population.[4] This is still a relatively young population. On the other hand, in 1991 only 1.2% of the BME population was of pensionable age, compared to nearly one in five of the white population. Consequently, there are few households of retired older people from these groups. This has its impact on housing needs and, as the population grows older, will lead to changes in the housing patterns and types of households encountered by healthcare workers.

Due to migration and social factors, the BME communities are clustered in large urban centres – particularly in London, the West Midlands and Yorkshire.[3] Within each of these urban locations, the majority of the BME population are found in 'inner-city' or less well-favoured areas. These were close to employment opportunities and availability of affordable housing for the first migrants. In public debate these areas tend to be described in negative terms, as 'ghettos', which may hinder 'integration'. There are, however, good reasons for the patterns, which in many cases did not arise out of choice.

Racial discrimination in the 1950s played a key role in restricting the choices on offer, and communities grew up where housing for sale or rent could be found.[5] These areas have subsequently grown and become stable due to availability of community facilities, including shops selling 'ethnic foods', religious centres and health centres that employ professionals who speak the language of the community. The common feature of 'suburbanisation', as middle-class families move to richer areas on the outskirts of cities, has been less marked among BME communities, particularly because of the fear of racial harassment in such areas. This is reinforced by the fact that house prices in the inner-city areas have not kept pace with the market elsewhere. Consequently, whilst almost one in five of the white population lives in areas classified as 'rural, resort and retirement', less than 4% of the BME population does. These differences in location have their consequences for healthcare provision, particularly in planning services to meet specific needs.

Both within cities and between them there are other effects arising from the history of early migration, as different minority groups tended to settle in different areas (*see* Box 4.1).[3] For example, Coventry has a predominantly Punjabi Indian community, Leicester a large population of Gujarati origin who settled there following expulsion from East Africa, and Tower Hamlets is home to a large Bangladeshi community. Even within cities such as Birmingham,[6] certain streets or neighbourhoods have become known as the community of a particular group, often following the process of 'chain migration', whereby people tend to settle in areas selected by earlier migrant members of their family or community of origin, close to friends and facilities designed around their language and cultural needs. This was often reinforced by the recruitment policy of employers and by restrictions in the availability of council housing and other rented accommodation.

Box 4.1: Location

- Ethnic minorities tend to live in areas where people of similar origin 'cluster'.
- BME communities are associated with 'inner-city' areas in major cities.
- Historical racial discrimination, and present-day fear of racial attack, keep these patterns from changing.

It is known that South Asian (Indian, Pakistani, Bangladeshi) communities prefer certain core urban areas for safety, closeness to community, family and friends, places of worship and ethnic shopping facilities.[7] Community resources enhanced by physical proximity are at times seen as more important than property quality. These resources might even include access to a medical practice where staff speak required languages, or recognise cultural needs (including being responsive to issues around gender and religious observance). Housing has therefore been inclined to be fairly restricted spatially, with moves tending either to be within existing areas of settlement or to contiguous neighbourhoods, where the move is to a more prestigious location.[8]

It is speculated that the concentration of these groups will continue, if not intensify. There is, however, some local evidence that more economically successful members of minority communities have bought 'middle-class' housing on developments in inner-city locations, thereby beginning a virtuous circle of urban regeneration (which may also attract white young professionals back into such areas). For a number of BME communities there appears to be greater flexibility of location amongst car owners, the young and better off, although most moves would still be within reach of the community. Location flexibility tends to be inspired by confidence in the opportunities of the owner-occupied sector and constrained by fear of crime and racist harassment in social housing, especially local authority housing. Surveys have reported that BME respondents opt for 'inner-city' areas as offering preferred shopping facilities, cultural and religious benefits, but at the expense of an apparently poorer urban physical environment than elsewhere in the city.[9,10] Inner urban residents valued 'the safety and comfort gained from living amongst one's own community'.

Refugees represent a particular case and have tended to concentrate in London, although national programmes, such as that for the East African Asians in the 1960s and the recent refugee dispersal system, have tried to disperse asylum seekers across the country.[11] The experience of the Vietnamese community shows that most groups eventually tried to move back to London where they could find mutual support and services designed for their cultural and language needs.[10] Similar patterns and processes are likely to emerge in relation to more recent flows of refugees (such as those of Kurdish, Bosnian and Afghanistan origin) unless strong attractions are developed in the regions to support them and maintain their sense of community. Such processes have developed in some places, and explain why there are relatively large communities of Somalis in cities such as Liverpool, Cardiff and Bristol.

Migration of members of BME groups can take different forms. Recently, there has been significant migration into Birmingham of nationals of the Netherlands and other European Union countries who are of Somali origin. This is confirmed by researchers in the Netherlands, who found that migrants wish to be in a larger community of Somalis, expect benefits from being in a country with a major language, and expect to experience less discrimination and exclusion than in the Netherlands.[12]

Household type

A critical factor in healthcare, and in planning for future health needs, is an understanding of household formation and types (*see* Table 4.1). There is a strong stereotype in much existing literature that 'typical' ethnic minority households are large, with many children, that 'West Indian' or African-Caribbean households frequently have a single (female) parent and that South Asians prefer to live in 'extended' (multi-generational) households. This pattern is changing. For example, as the proportion of older people in the South Asian communities rises, there are increasing numbers of older people living alone, in sheltered accommodation and in flats adjacent to, rather than part of, family homes.[13] This has considerable implications for the potential for informal care provision.

Table 4.1: Household type in 1991

Ethnic group	Household size (average)	% households 'one-parent'	% households 'lone pensioner'	% households 'large family' (3+ adults)
White	2.43	4.0	15.6	16.7
Black Caribbean	2.52	16.4	5.3	18.6
Indian	3.80	7.0	2.0	35.4
Pakistani	4.81	4.9	0.9	35.7
Bangladeshi	5.34	1.4	0.7	38.7

Source: Owen[14]

There is debate on the breakdown in the extended family system with greater tendency towards the formation of smaller, separate households.[15,16] Karn *et al.*[17] noted amongst the Pakistani and Bangladeshi communities in Manchester that: 'while the extended family is likely to remain a key social unit ... and one whose needs are not adequately being met, pressure is also building up for more separate living arrangements'. The break-up of extended families will become a self-fulfilling prophecy if insufficient larger dwellings are not provided. A 'forced' retention of the extended unit (i.e. one resulting from external material forces) could only result in increased overcrowding with its attendant risks to health.

Housing tenure and amenities

The 1991 Census showed that two-thirds of the national population were owner occupiers – and a further quarter lived in local authority or Housing Association 'social housing'. For minority ethnic communities, less than half the African-Caribbean population owned their own home, while more than three out of four people of South Asian origin did so. However, more than one in three Bangladeshis lived in local authority accommodation, and only 44% were owner occupiers. Nearly one in five Chinese people lived in privately rented housing, compared to 7% of the white population. While most analyses suggest that 'owner-occupied' housing is of better quality, this is not always the case, and for most minority ethnic groups ownership is often associated with poorer amenities, including lack of central heating, poor repair and other stresses associated with worse health outcome.[18] In the case of people with disabilities, this may also create problems in accessing local authority support for aids and adaptations or rehousing which would be less problematic for local authority tenants.[19] Groups in 'social housing' on the whole tend to have better levels of amenity compared to those in the private rented sector. However, ethnic minority households tend to be living in the poorest quality housing in each tenure.[20]

Evidence from the English House Condition Survey suggests that housing conditions for minority ethnic groups deteriorated nationally between 1991 and 1996.[20,21] Pakistani and Bangladeshi communities were particularly likely to fare badly. This is indicative of their high concentration in relatively poor quality owner-occupied dwellings and, in certain parts of the country, especially London, the presence of Bangladeshi households at the poorer end of the social rented sector. In many cases properties have been in such poor condition that renovation was never a realistic option, even if residents could afford it or grants were available. In cases where such invest-ment has been appropriate, research suggests that minority communities experienced disproportionate barriers; for example, in obtaining public funds to address disrepair and/or obtain Disabled Facilities Grants.[16,22]

The greatest divergence in the housing outcomes of white majority and certain minority ethnic communities, however, relates to levels of overcrowding. South Asian households, and those of Bangladeshi origin in particular, tend to be larger than those in other communi-ties, both minority and majority.[15,23] Overcrowding stems primarily from the inability to afford appropriate space, but also reflects the shortage of larger properties in the public sector. The Survey of English Housing[20] shows over 25% of Bangladeshi and 20% of Pakistani households as being 'overcrowded', compared to 1% of white households, 7% of Black/African-Caribbean households and 8% of Indian households. As described in Chapter 2, overcrowding leads to higher levels of cross-infection and respiratory disease, possi-bly to higher levels of domestic accident, frequently to increased mental stress, and is generally thought to be a predictor of poor health for all members of the household.

The worst outcome in terms of housing stress is possibly homeless-ness (see Box 4.2). However, there are no national figures or research into homelessness among BME populations. Limited research (see Chapter 3) conducted in London has suggested that the patterns of homelessness among young black men are distinctive, as they tend to be assisted by sequential temporary accommodation among friends and family, as may be the case for other minority ethnic groups, leading to increased numbers of 'concealed households' and further (but hidden) overcrowding. This is possibly a response to fear of racial attack 'on the streets' as much as a case of 'caring for their own'[24] but represents another source of stress and potential ill health among the group.

Box 4.2: Housing stress and disabilities

- Homelessness.
- Overcrowding.
- Lack of amenities.
- Racial attack.

There is a strong association between health and socio-economic status.[25] Largely because of this, those of Chinese, African Asian and Indian origin exhibit a similar level of morbidity to that of whites, and the Bangladeshis, Pakistanis and Caribbeans fare worse than whites.[26] There are few national data on patterns of disability in minority ethnic communities. Data from Bradford demonstrate particularly high levels of chronic long-term illness and impairment.[23] These are also reflected in the national census data which show higher than expected levels for 'long-term limiting illness',[14] despite the generally younger age profile of minority ethnic households. However, as these data cannot be linked to individual circumstances they are difficult to interpret. There is some evidence that the earlier industrial experiences of minority ethnic workers in dangerous industrial settings (such as boiler-making and foundries) has led to higher levels of industrial disability – if people are aware of their entitlements,[27] this may express itself in higher levels of demand for mobility assistance or housing adaptations.

There is evidence of extremely low take-up rates of social services support amongst minority communities.[13] It tends to be family and friends who assume the role of carer in the event of chronic sickness or disability, rather than statutory or even voluntary sector agencies, reflecting an emphasis on informal, rather than formal, care provision.[28] The predicted steep growth in the numbers of African-Caribbean and Asian older people is not only likely to increase the demand for community care and sheltered housing, but is also likely to alter the ratio of younger to older people and consequently the potential to arrange informal care. This may provide the social housing sector with new opportunities or challenges, as well as having implications for planning health and social care.

Minority ethnic communities have experienced a number of difficulties in gaining sensitive assessments of their care needs. Elders are disproportionately affected due to misconceptions about the services available, compounded by assumptions on the part of mainstream health and housing providers about the absence of need amongst this group. Social care providers can only be seen to be conforming to Best Value principles[29] if they respond to this diversity by making their accommodation and services accessible to the whole community. This means moving away from a global model of need based on majority white communities.

Implications for primary care organisations, GPs and healthcare providers

All primary care organisations, such as trusts, and professionals working to deliver healthcare services need to take careful account of their local demographic population profile and assure themselves that they have information on the local patterns of minority ethnic settlement and community. This will help them to predict and meet medical, cultural, religious and gender-specific needs, and may help to ensure that supports are in place when needs arise.

The most commonly required specific resource is that of language support. Interpreter provision is expensive and may be difficult to obtain.[30] However, it is an element of the Government's funding formula [Simon Fradd, General Practitioners Committee, personal communication] and should not be denied on the grounds of 'costs'. Indeed, as in the legal services, there is growing belief that this may be a 'human rights' issue. Service providers and planners need information on the current patterns of home-spoken languages (which may be available through schools and education authorities) and should be aware that as people of non-English-speaking background grow older, they may lose their acquired facility in English.

Provision of such specialised support services is, in general, made easier by concentration of specific minority groups. Similarly, from the point of view of the practitioner, a preference to live close to community religious facilities and family members makes it more likely that older and disabled people will have access to community support. This should not, however, be taken for granted, and agencies and family members may require additional support or training in the support and health needs of members of their community with particular health conditions.

Finally, it is important to recognise that the patterns and profiles of the minority ethnic communities are changing. As families develop and grow up, new needs and expectations emerge, which may not be met by current housing provision or local economic opportunities. Older people lose acquired facilities, and younger ones may move away. Spouses may come from abroad and require familiarisation with UK services and procedures. Primary care needs to reflect changing needs of the BME populations it serves.

References

1 Johnson MRD (2002) Ethnic diversity in social context. In: J Kai (ed.) *Ethnicity, Health and Primary Care*. Oxford University Press, Oxford.

2 www.legislation.hmso.gov.uk/acts/acts2000/20000034.htm

3 Gill PS, Kai J, Bhopal RS and Wild S (2002) *Black and Minority Ethnic Groups*. Part of the *Healthcare Needs Assessment: the epidemiologically based needs assessment reviews, Third Series*. Available online at:
http://hcna.radcliffe-online.com/bemgframe.htm

4 Scott A, Pearce D and Goldblatt P (2001) The sizes and characteristics of the minority ethnic populations of Great Britain: latest estimates. *Popul Trends*. 105:6–15.

5 Johnson MRD (1987) Housing as a process of racial discrimination. In: S Smith and J Mercer (eds) *New Perspectives on Race and Housing in Britain*. Centre for Housing Research, Glasgow University.

6 Owen D and Johnson MRD (1996) Ethnic minorities in the Midlands. In: P Ratcliffe (ed.) *Social Geography and Ethnicity in Britain: geographical spread, spatial concentration and internal migration*. HMSO, London.

7 Tomlins R (1999) Housing experiences of minority ethnic communities in Britain. *Bibliographies in Ethnic Relations*. **15**. Centre for Research in Ethnic Relations, Coventry.

8 Phillips D and Karn V (1992) Race and housing in a property owning democracy. *New Community*. **18**:355–69.

9 Ratcliffe P, Harrison ML, Hogg R *et al.* (2001) *Breaking Down the Barriers: improving Asian access to Social Rented Housing*. Chartered Institute of Housing, Coventry.

10 Tomlins R, Johnson MRD, Line B *et al.* (2000) *Building Futures. Meeting the needs of our Vietnamese communities*. An Viet Housing Association, London.

11 www.legislation.hmso.gov.uk/acts1999/19990033.htm

12 Van onze verslaggever (2002) Voor Somaliers lonkt het groene gras elders. *De Volkskrant*, Amsterdam, 4 June.

13 Ahmad WIU and Atkin K (1996) *Race and Community Care*. Open University Press, Buckingham.

14 Owen D (1993) *Minorities in Great Britain. Housing and Family Characteristics. Census Statistical Paper 4*. Centre for Research in Ethnic Relations, National Ethnic Minority Data Archive, Coventry.

15 Kempson E (1993) *Overcrowding in Bangladeshi Households. A case study of Tower Hamlets*. Policy Studies Institute, London.

16 Law I, Davies J, Phillips D and Harrison M (1996) *Equity and Difference: racial and ethnic inequalities in housing needs and housing investment in Leeds*. University of Leeds, Leeds.

17 Karn V, Mian S, Brown M and Dale A (1999) *Tradition, Change and Diversity. Understanding the housing needs of minority ethnic groups in Manchester*. Housing Corporation, London.

18 Cooper H (2002) Investigating socio-economic explanations for gender and ethnic inequalities in health. *Soc Sci Med.* **54:**693–706.

19 Johnson MRD, Wright A, Jeffcoat M and Petherick R (1996) Local authority occupational therapy services and ethnic minority clients. *Br J Occup Ther.* **59:**109–14.

20 www.housing.odpm.gov.uk/research/ehcs

21 Tomlins R and James D (2001) *Black and Minority Ethnic Communities: key data.* Sector Study 11. Housing Corporation, London.

22 Ratcliffe P (1992) Renewal, regeneration and 'race': issues in urban policy. *New Community.* **18(3):**387–400.

23 Ratcliffe P (1996) *Race and Housing in Bradford.* Bradford Housing Forum, Bradford.

24 Chahal K (1999) *Minority Ethnic Homelessness in London.* NHS Executive, London Regional Office.

25 Acheson D (1998) *Independent Inquiry into Inequalities in Health.* The Stationery Office, London.

26 Modood T, Berthoud R, Lakey J *et al.* (1997) *Ethnic Minorities in Britain. Diversity and disadvantage.* Policy Studies Institute, London.

27 Ahmad WIU (2000) *Ethnicity, Disability and Chronic Illness.* Open University Press, Buckingham.

28 University of Salford (1996) *The Housing Needs of the Asian and African/Caribbean Community of Peterborough.* University of Salford, Salford.

29 www.housing.odpm.gov.uk/factsheet/bestv/index.htm

30 Jones D and Gill P (1998) Breaking down language barriers. *BMJ.* **316:**1476–80.

Chapter 5

Collaboration for meeting housing needs

Murray Hawtin

Introduction

The connection between housing and health has been recognised for well over a hundred years, with a housing policy emerging from attempts by Victorian environmental health activists to address urban slums. Although the health service subsequently proceeded to focus on an individualistic medical approach, the work of environmental health agencies continues to be an important aspect in tackling poor housing conditions in the private sector. It is generally recognised (*see* Chapter 2) that an adequate supply of decent housing, in whatever tenure, is essential for a good quality life – socially, emotionally as well as physically, and may also reduce the reliance on residential care, improve employment prospects of its occupiers and help alleviate poverty. Conversely, the poorest sections of society have the worst health and live in the worst housing with poor access to adequate health and social care.[1-3]

The first two chapters examined the links between housing and health policy and healthcare; this chapter provides an overview of approaches that housing has made in addressing health issues through the provision and management of accommodation and support. Housing and support is focused on people who are especially vulnerable (physically or mentally) and the following section examines the part housing has played in the development of community care and the growing awareness of the need for collaboration between agencies. Such collaboration has not been easy. Over the last two decades successive governments focused their health and welfare policies on individual responsibility and attempted to reduce general-need provision of state services in favour of a residualised market driven approach to welfare provision. The White Paper *Health of the Nation*,[4] for example, emphasised a narrow range of key risk behaviours, including smoking, alcohol consumption and exercise, but showed little concern with linking poor health to wider environmental factors such as poverty and housing. Given the divergence of professional approaches of these services which began early this century, the emphasis on an individualistic model of intervention and a monetarist climate, it was not surprising that studies in the 1990s showed that collaboration between the relevant agencies was highly problematic.[5,6]

The current government, however, recognises the importance of collaboration between services such as health, housing and social care, demonstrated by the White Paper *Our Healthier Nation*[7] as well as through Health Action Zones (HAZs), primary care trusts and Health Improvement Programmes (HImPs). Policy initiatives such as these, where housing can contribute to a more holistic view towards improving health, may take time to change the prevailing cultures and practices of welfare services. Despite the many, and often deep-seated, barriers to collaboration, many agencies, or at least individuals within agencies do, however, co-operate in planning and delivering an effective service that integrates both housing and health.

Housing provision and management

One of the major contributions social housing has made to the care of people has been through special schemes. From the 1960s local authorities have provided housing specifically for older people, such as sheltered housing, and the majority of mobility housing is owned by local authorities. In addition, housing associations have provided for special needs with many being dedicated to providing only special needs housing. Since the early 1980s, however, the development of new local authority and sheltered housing has declined dramatically, affecting disabled people in particular.

Meanwhile, housing authorities are becoming progressively more involved in a spectrum of care activities including the provision of accommodation which does not fit easily into the category of 'home' or 'institution', such as core and cluster and group living schemes, as well as providing central alarm systems and floating support.

Some people have argued that providing for 'special needs' diverts attention from the need to provide affordable, appropriate and flexible housing within mainstream provision.[8] Furthermore, many people, including those in Britain's disability movement, have argued that living a 'normal' life requires a political focus on 'ordinary' housing with support (such as adaptations, day care, home nursing, etc.) relocated to users' own homes. Well-designed, ordinary housing (or housing that can be adapted and with appropriate support), can reduce or even remove care needs, helping many to stay in their homes. Housing needs to be suitable for both the person being cared for and the needs of any carer. The concept of 'lifetime homes' has been developed to go beyond basic requirements and cater for the changing needs of households throughout their lifetime. Such homes may include accessible doorways, wheelchair accessibility, downstairs toilet and scope for adding a stair lift. Some people argue that as the additional costs are small, compared with adapting an existing house for a disabled person or providing residential care, such standards should be applied in a proportion of all new private and public sector housing.[9]

Although ordinary housing may have limitations for some people, regarding 'ordinary' housing as a starting point can potentially make a significant difference to contextualising and developing care. While the majority of disabled people, or those with care needs, live in local authority housing, there is little evidence of government support for expanding general social housing. Indeed, successive governments' determination to control public borrowing and reduce public expenditure has hit public housing extensively. Over two million of the better dwellings within local authorities have been sold, leaving councils with the less desirable properties, and years of restrictions on local authority spending on housing has resulted in a massive backlog of repairs and maintenance. Consequently, such policies, along with care in the community, have led to council housing becoming residualised with an image of being 'second best' or of only being fit for those unable or unwilling to 'help themselves'.

Inadequacies within mainstream housing provision may lead those needing care and support to enter residential care or other supported housing schemes,[10,11] or even to become homeless.[12] However, local housing agencies are dealing increasingly with more vulnerable tenants, many of whom do not receive care, often because their needs are not deemed sufficient to warrant scarce resources. Housing managers are often the first to be aware of tenants in distress and provide support beyond basic housing management, including monitoring, support and advice. Although the service offered to tenants with community care needs varies considerably both within and between housing departments, Clapham and Franklin[13] identified a number of roles that housing management plays (*see* Box 5.1).

Box 5.1: Roles of housing managers

- Intensive housing management.
- Liaison with social services over community care, children at risk or the mentally ill.
- Helping to develop community projects such as 'good neighbour schemes.
- Arranging adaptations for people with disabilities.
- Welfare aspects of wardens' work.

Housing and vulnerable people

Within society there are particular groups of people for whom the combination of housing, medical and social problems are of great concern. These include the homeless/travellers; refugees/asylum seekers; those who have a mental illness; those who have a physical problem due to age or illness such as HIV and AIDS; and those who are vulnerable because of their poverty or young age without support from family and friends. The relationship between homelessness and health (*see* Chapter 3) epitomises the centrality of housing in meeting people's health and social care needs. The number of people who are disabled and frail due to age is increasing whilst the numbers of appropriate residential places are falling, hospitals are being encouraged to discharge people as early as possible to free up bed spaces and many psychiatric institutions have been closed. The essential links between housing and health have therefore been brought into focus through these issues and the attempt to solve them through the care in the community policy.

The 1950s saw the start of a shift from caring for people in large institutions to providing care in a 'community' setting. Many long-stay hospitals, especially psychiatric ones, began to be closed and the residents resettled in the community. This policy change, combined with an increasing elderly population in need of care, necessitated a significant expansion in residential care provision. The corresponding rise in cost to the social security budget necessitated a strategic response which was addressed by the Griffiths Report.[14] Griffiths minimised the link between housing and both community care and the medical service. However, after considerable pressure from professionals and academics, the subsequent White Paper *Caring for People* conceded that 'housing is a vital component of community care and often the key to independent living'.[15] Following the 1990 NHS and Community Care Act, the Department of the Environment and the Department of Health produced a joint circular entitled 'Housing and Community Care',[16] which stressed the importance of adequate housing in community care and the necessity for inter-agency collaboration. It also acknowledged that housing needs arising from community care assessments should be met by local housing strategies and submissions. 'The Government wants housing to play a full part, working together with social service departments and health authorities so that each effectively discharge their responsibilities.'[16] Such advice was emphasised in a later joint circular[17] along with examples of good practice and indications of possible approaches for housing, social services and health authorities.[18]

These, and many similar statements originating not only from central government but also from the NHS and local authorities, are based on community care policies that assume vulnerable people are able to live in 'normal' healthy homes. However, in reality, accessible accommodation, usually provided by local authorities, is often only available on unpopular, poor quality estates, which is neither healthy nor safe. Furthermore, most people within the community care categories characteristically suffer from a range of inter-related problems, including access to sufficient personal resources, problems which are the responsibility of a proliferation of different agencies including voluntary organisations. Community care assessment systems, however, do not work well for those with such multiple needs, especially for those who are homeless. The National Health Service and Community Care Act 1990 assumes that people who are to be assessed for community care have some form of accommodation.

Issues in collaboration between housing and health

Despite this plethora of injunctions, recommendations and good practice advice concerning collaboration between housing and care agencies, most research suggests that progress has at best been slow and in many respects disappointing. Goss and Kent[6] found that, although there is some inter-agency working across the boundaries between housing and health, it was not high on the agenda, and that the focus of health and housing organisations is more inward than outward, resulting in collaboration being patchy. Arblaster *et al.*[5] also found little evidence of three-way links between housing, health and social care agencies; links between social care and health were reasonably good but tended to leave out housing. They concluded that:

- there is a widespread lack of understanding of other agencies – their roles and responsibilities, boundaries between them and the constraints that each other is working under
- organisations are often unsure of the services provided by, and personnel within, other agencies
- where collaboration at strategic level exists it is often not implemented or mirrored at service delivery level
- there are general difficulties in communications and sharing information at the level of service delivery between agency workers, including false expectations and mistrust of other professional groups
- user involvement is unsuccessful at the strategic level and agencies rarely provide a co-ordinated inter-agency response to user demands.

The Audit Commission's report on the role of housing in community care also concluded that 'too many people fall through the net' because of 'poor collaboration between housing, social services and health authorities'.[19] Exploring the causes of this, Arblaster *et al.*[5] identified a range of national and local factors influencing inter-agency working, which may be classified as four inter-relating groups.

- The broad macro context (such as demographic trends, economic factors and political priorities).
- The means whereby policies are implemented and delivered (legislation, resources and links between government departments).
- The structure of agencies (the range of organisational types, the separation of purchasing and provision, geographic boundaries and local political priorities).

- Organisational operation of agencies (agency objectives, organisational structure and style, and professional values and skills).

The broad context within which local housing and care agencies operate is largely given. National and local government operates within priorities that are partly determined by factors such as demographic trends and economic constraints, and partly by party policy. These priorities affect the work of local agencies both directly, by fixing the legal and financial framework, and indirectly, by creating the policy climate in which these agencies are able to operate.

Collaboration is also affected by the extent to which government programmes and policies clearly assist co-ordination. Where inter-agency programmes such as the Single Regeneration Budget and the HAZs are established, bringing together the resources and policies of a number of government departments, local agencies are more easily encouraged to work together. Conversely, within government department programmes that are not so co-ordinated, local agencies find it problematic to establish effective links. Indeed, until recently there has been neither a clear agenda nor co-ordination of government programmes at the national level within which local agencies could operate collectively.[19–23]

Recent changes in the structure of government and voluntary organisations have influenced the nature of inter-agency collaboration and new working relationships.[5,24,25] Local government, as well as central government, departments have historically worked independently with little thought given to the impact of their development on other departments. However, a number of recent administrative developments have affected departmental isolation including the review of single- and dual-tier local authorities and changes to government boundaries; changes in the boundaries in responsibilities of health authorities and other health agencies; the separation of purchasers from providers of housing, social care and health; and the increased role of the voluntary and independent sectors such as the transfer of large numbers of council houses to housing associations. The expanding 'modernising local government' agenda has set changes in motion with local authorities encouraged to become community leaders.[26] Some authorities have combined their housing and social service departments, although the effectiveness of this depends on links being forged at all levels from political and chief executive through to housing managers and social workers.

Effective inter-agency collaboration is also related to organisational operation which is, to some extent, influenced by differences in professional structures, philosophies, culture, language and training, as well as agency aims and objectives.[13,27] As medical care and housing professional groups and agencies developed as separate areas of public policy, their goals and priorities, and the links between the professional groups, have weakened.[28] Furthermore, there is a tendency for professional interests to become entrenched and those at senior policy-making levels may see little professional incentives to forge better working links with those in other professional groups. They may even see the closer involvement with other professionals as 'undermining their role as an expert'.[28]

Opportunities for further collaboration

In order for collaboration to be effective, all the above factors need to be addressed. The current government, in recognising the need for a strong policy context for collaboration, has proposed and initiated a range of developments designed to encourage health to work closely with other agencies including housing. However, before such policies can be implemented effectively, Arblaster et al.[30] have argued that five key elements of collaboration need to be addressed:

- a conceptual understanding of the overall functions of agencies
- an understanding of what agencies do in practice, how they function on a day-to-day basis
- a recognition of mutual compatibility
- clarification of relationships between agencies – including effective communication and trust between agencies

- additional resources, linked to the estimated costs of care support and social housing.

Despite the slow development of inter-agency activity, there has been a growing number of innovative examples of good practice and diversity of collaborative schemes, although many have tended to be ad hoc and are the exception rather than the rule. Nevertheless, these show that there is a willingness to try to overcome the range of barriers outlined above.[30–32]

Joint planning and commissioning

Under previous governments, housing felt marginalised at all levels of joint planning and often felt left out of joint commissioning processes. This was partly due to marginalisation by other agencies (particularly health and social services), partly through an unwillingness of housing agencies to become involved, and partly through other structural problems outlined above.[5,33,34] Planning of services was based almost entirely on aggregating individuals' needs assessed by services in isolation, which in reality made rationing more easy. The New Labour agenda, in attempting to challenge social exclusion and develop sustainable communities, now seeks to address a wider range of collective needs focusing on managing provider networks and including users. The broad changes to increase the scope and nature of joint working arrangements between the NHS and local authorities are found in the consultation paper *Partners in Action*,[35] backed up by the Health Service Circular *Integration of Joint Finance Allocation 1999/2000*.[36] The aims of the proposals are to attempt to bring local authorities and health authorities closer together through:

- pooling budgets
- giving a lead commissioning role

• integrating providers more fully.

The government White Paper *The New NHS: modern, dependable*[37] outlined their plans for HImPs, which are seen as a national priority. Government guidance for developing them was set out in the circular *Health Improvement Programmes: planning for better health and better health care*, and although there is only one reference to housing, health authorities have a clear role in involving housing agencies in developing HImPs in their area. Furthermore, in an attempt to address the issues of the complexities of funding support for people with special needs and the problems of inter-agency working, the DSS produced a consultation document, *Supporting People: a new policy and funding framework for support services*.[38] The document proposes that the local authority becomes responsible for providing support needs of people whatever tenure they are in, and also that a Commissioning Committee is established within the local authority area composed of representatives from housing, probation and social services who will need to collaborate over a merged budget for managing and supporting special needs groups.

The precise nature of needs for which local housing and care agencies must cater will depend on local variations in demographic trends, knowledge of which will depend on the amount of local research and information. Collecting and subsequent planning based on such information should involve all relevant agencies. There are previous examples of good practice where housing is involved in health and care planning, particularly through mechanisms such as locality planning, special needs housing forums and primary care groups.[33,34] Joint approaches to housing needs assessment are also becoming more common; both Manchester and Leeds are good examples of these.[30,39,40] Watson and Conway[41] detail one way to approach the process of developing a joint strategy in their useful addition to the subject, and good examples of joint commissioning are beginning to develop, such as that between the Royal Borough of Kensington and Chelsea and Westminster Health Authority.[42] Castlemilk Public Health Review, commissioned by the Castlemilk Partnership and Greater Glasgow Health Board, aimed to assess local health challenges, identify opportunities and recommend action to the Health Working Group which includes the housing department.[43]

Multi-agency programmes

Disabled people's ability to live a 'normal' life may be regarded as related closely to their integration within the community with which they wish to be identified. Projects taking a holistic approach to residents' needs – being not just housing or health needs in isolation – attempt to bring together all the relevant agencies and residents working and living in an area. All members of the community may be viewed as potential users, carers or volunteers, and in this way the community has the capacity to become a 'caring community'. Such a community development approach seeks to include the wider community in developing solutions to healthcare problems through devising their own agenda, developing their own initiatives and managing the delivery of services themselves in a way that meets their own specific needs. Using such a focus the Government's Social Exclusion Unit has established a New Deal for Regeneration programme that is aimed at tackling around 20 of what the Unit calls 'the country's worst estates'. The timescale they have set for the action teams covers the next 10 to 20 years. Regeneration and housing programmes will be brought together locally to enhance economic and employment opportunities.

Health Action Zones have also been established by the Government to address causes of poor health and are based on a partnership approach to help reduce health inequality. Such proposals involve pooling budgets between agencies and developing more integrated forms of working. Each Zone will range from five to ten years, encouraging a longer-term approach to development. The first 11 Zones were established in 1998 following competitive bids. Plymouth HAZ aims to reduce homelessness and the number of children living in unsuitable housing. Tyne and Wear HAZ has set up a home insulation scheme and improvements to older people's accommodation, and in Sandwell the HAZ aimed to set up an energy-saving project, a healthy living advice centre and build 1000 environmentally friendly dwellings.

Inter-agency projects

In addition to programmes established to address the wide range of needs within a community, collaboration between housing and social care agencies may operate within specific projects set up by any one or more of those agencies. Such projects may concern the plight of vulnerable groups with multiple health or community care needs, such as people with alcohol- and drug-related problems, people with HIV or AIDS, or people who may present as homeless but have an underlying care need. The following are examples of a few areas that have established such projects.

Interdisciplinary teams have been established such as those in Watford, Cardiff's Ely Hospital, Liverpool and Hounslow.[30] The housing association Circle 33, for example, has a central team of housing and support workers with specialist expertise and knowledge each with a small caseload of tenants identified as causing concern.[44] The Community Mental Health Care Trust in South Devon allocates two people to the housing department to assist them with tenants with mental health problems.[30] In other instances agencies have recognised the need to address the issues of lack of knowledge, understanding and trust between agencies. Inter-agency groups in Wolverhampton, Salford and Durham have, for example, undertaken joint training.[30] Other areas, such as Bromley and Salford,[30] have established protocols for joint working. An innovative inter-agency project in Leeds, established by the City Council and incorporating representatives from health and social care agencies, produces a regular informative bulletin called the 'Communiqué'.

There are growing numbers of projects involving hospital discharges or admissions. Cardiff's Ely Hospital has a multidisciplinary team containing officers from the social services, housing services department and the hospital which is concerned with the resettlement of people with learning difficulties from the long-stay hospital; accommodation is tailor-made to meet specific individual needs.[30] In Manchester the Discharge Planning Service was launched in 1997. It is a joint initiative by the Mental Health Directorate, the health authority and Manchester Social Services, which works to ensure that all hospital inpatients have a discharge plan. In addition, the co-ordinator inspects housing schemes to ensure the appropriateness of referrals and establish a working relationship with the staff.[43] Another resettlement team operates in Hounslow.[30] Two projects were established in Birmingham that provided grants to improve the homes of patients nominated by GPs on the basis that this is likely to reduce the risk of admissions to hospitals. Funding for the schemes came through the Joint Funding mechanism.[30]

Housing-related issues faced by disabled people are being addressed by the Disabled Persons Housing Service (DPHS) which aims to co-ordinate advice and service delivery from a one-stop shop approach. DPHSs may be provided by independent agencies such as that in Lothian funded by local government, the health board, the Scottish Office, Scottish Homes, charitable trusts and the private sector, or provided by a housing association such as Walbrook Housing Association in Derby.[43] Wakefield's Adaptations and Disability Unit is funded jointly by health, housing and social services. It is staffed by occupational therapists who assess people's disability including patients being discharged from hospital; provide and check on equipment including chairlifts; are involved in housing allocations; and undertake satisfaction surveys to monitor the quality of building services.[43] The supported accommodation team in Glasgow has improved a number of houses aimed at people suffering from HIV and developed supported units for them.[42] Many older people live in poor housing conditions where adaptations and technical aids can make caring easier or help them remain independent. Home improvement agencies and supported living schemes such as *Care And Repair* usually work alongside health and housing agencies; Sheffield's Stay Put scheme operates a home safety scheme jointly with the health authority's Health Promotion Centre.[30]

Health services also have a key role to play in allocating social housing and assessing the appropriateness of housing and support. In Kirklees a Medical Advisory Service assists applicants in deciding the best way to meet their housing needs, and the Health for All Strategy Group in Rotherham receives medical policies with reference to medical needs.[31] The Royal Borough of Kensington and Chelsea employs a nurse, and the Mole Valley District Council an occupational therapist, to assist with medical assessments for rehousing. In Newcastle a health adviser, an occupational therapist and a community psychiatric nurse have been seconded to the City Council's housing department from the health authority to advise on an applicant's medical condition when housing officers are deciding on health implications of moving a tenant. Fairer medical assessments and more appropriate allocations have resulted from this greater understanding by housing officers.[43]

Conclusions

Within the last decade the process of linking health, housing and social care became focused around the introduction of community care reforms, although a range of factors prevent a fully co-ordinated approach to environmental and health service provision. The Acheson inquiry into health inequalities[45] made a number of recommendations based on the belief in a social and environmental approach to health. It recommended developing policies that aim to:

- improve the availability of social housing for poorer people (alongside environmental improvement, planning and design)
- improve housing provision and access to healthcare for people who are homeless
- improve the quality of housing, including heating and insulation systems as well as regulations aimed to reduce home accidents

- reduce the fear of crime and violence, creating a safer living environment.

New Labour accelerated collaboration through a 'joined-up' approach, with their emphasis on a holistic approach aimed more at the community than solutions based on an individualistic medical model. This has resulted in a range of opportunities and initiatives that Acheson has categorised as 'upstream' and 'downstream'.[45] The upstream initiatives focus on promotion and health improvement where social housing agencies become collaborators in health improvement planning, identifying needs and co-ordinating regeneration schemes. Within downstream initiatives, with their focus on treatment and care, housing agencies have an important role to play in providing essential health infrastructure including healthy, safe accommodation, environments and support, as well as being main collaborators within initiatives such as home improvement agencies, floating support and tenant care support schemes, and hospital discharge schemes.

However, despite the increasing good practice based on exhortations for agencies to collaborate, many professionals are concerned that vulnerable people could suffer because of the inadequacies of housing policies. People needing support or care are usually the most vulnerable and often the most powerless in society, lacking collective political representation and having a weak lobbying position. The impact of this lack of political leverage affects their entire situations, including their need for housing and care resources. As the great majority of care users rely on social housing, the devastating cuts to housing funding over the last two decades have had a significant impact on such groups and severely undermine the potential for housing to serve as a positive care intervention.

References

1 Boardman B (1991) *Fuel Poverty: from cold homes to affordable warmth*. Belhaven, London.

2 Curtis S (1991) Residential location as a gateway to health care. In: S Smith, R Knill-Jones and A McGuckin (eds) *Housing for Health*. Longman, Harlow.

3 Arblaster L and Hawtin M (1993) *Health, Housing and Social Policy*. Socialist Health Association, London.

4 Department of Health (1992) *The Health of the Nation: a strategy for health in England.* HMSO, London.

5 Arblaster L, Conway J, Foreman A and Hawtin M (1996) *Asking the Impossible: interagency working to address the housing, health and social care needs of people in ordinary housing.* Policy Press/Joseph Rowntree Foundation, Bristol.

6 Goss S and Kent C (1995) *Health and Housing: Working Together. A review of the extent of inter-agency working.* Policy Press/Joseph Rowntree Foundation, Bristol.

7 DoH (1997) *Our Healthier Nation: a contract for health.* Cm 3854. The Stationery Office, London.

8 Means R and Smith R (1994) *Community Care: policy and practice.* Macmillan, Basingstoke.

9 Cobbold C (1996) *A Cost Benefit Analysis of Lifetime Homes.* York Publishing Services Ltd, York.

10 Sinclair I (1998) *Bridging Two Worlds: social work and the elderly living alone.* Avebury, Aldershot.

11 Oldman C (1990) *Moving in Old Age: new directions in housing policies.* HMSO, London.

12 Office for Public Management (1992) *Assessment of the Housing Requirements of People with Special Needs Over the Next Decade.* Office for Public Management, London.

13 Clapham D and Franklin B (1994) *The Housing Management Contribution to Community Care.* Centre for Housing Research and Urban Studies, Glasgow.

14 Griffiths R (1998) *Community Care: agenda for action.* HMSO, London.

15 Department of Social Services (1989) *Caring for People: community care in the next decade and beyond.* HMSO, London.

16 Department of the Environment/Department of Health (1992) *Housing and Community Care Circular 10/92.* Department of the

Environment/Department of Health, London.

17 DoH/Department of the Environment, Transport and the Regions (1997) *Housing and Community Care: establishing a strategic framework.* DoH/DETR, London.

18 Means R, Brenton M, Harrison L and Heywood F (1997) *Making Partnerships Work in Community Care.* Policy Press, Bristol.

19 Audit Commission (1998) *Home Alone: the role of housing in community care.* Audit Commission, London.

20 Arnold P, Bochel HM, Broadhurst S and Page D (1993) *Community Care: the housing dimension.* Joseph Rowntree Foundation, York.

21 House of Commons Health Committee (1994) *Better Off in the Community? The care of people who are seriously mentally ill.* HMSO, London.

22 Harker M, Kilgallon B, Palmer J and Tickell C (1996) *Making Connections: policy and governance for community care.* National Federation of Housing Associations, London.

23 Fletcher P (1998) Care comes into focus. *Housing Today.* No. 85, 28 May.

24 Craig G (1993) *The Community Care Reforms and Local Government Change.* University of Humberside, School of Social and Professional Studies, Hull.

25 Craig G and Manthorpe J (1996) *Wiped Off the Map? Local government reorganisation and community care.* Papers in Social Research No. 5. University of Humberside, Hull.

26 DETR (1998) *Modernising Local Government.* The Stationery Office, London.

27 Wagner G (1988) *Residential Care, A Positive Choice.* HMSO, London.

28 Byrne DS, Harrison SP, Keithley J and McCarthy P (1986) *Health and Housing; the relationship between housing conditions and the health of council tenants.* Gower, Aldershot.

29 Reid B (1995) Interorganisational networks and the delivery of local housing services. *Housing Studies.* 10(2): 133–49.

30 Arblaster L, Conway J, Foreman A and Hawtin M (1998) *Achieving the Impossible? Collaboration in delivering housing, and*

community care. Policy Press, Bristol.

31 Association of Metropolitan Authorities (1997) *Housing and Health: getting it together.* AMA, London.

32 Means R, Brenton M, Harrison L and Heywood F (1997) *Making Partnerships Work in Community Care: a guide for practitioners in housing, health and social services.* DETR and DoH, London.

33 DoH (1994) *Implementing Caring For People: housing and homelessness.* HMSO, London.

34 Lund B and Foord M (1997) *Toward Integrated Living: housing strategies and community care.* Policy Press, Bristol.

35 DoH (1998) *Partners in Action.* HMSO, London.

36 DoH (1999) *Integration of Joint Finance Allocation 1999/2000.* Local Authority Social Services Letter (99)06. HMSO, London.

37 DoH (1997) *The New NHS: modern, dependable.* Cm 3807. The Stationery Office, London.

38 DSS (1999) *Supporting People: a new policy and funding framework for support services.* HMSO, London.

39 Watson L and Harker M (1993) *Community Care Planning: a model for housing need assessment.* National Federation of Housing Associations/Institute of Housing, London.

40 Foord M, Simic P, Bartles H and Ingham J (1999) Viable systems for planning: a case study on needs and planning for supported housing. *Housing and Support.* 2(3):12–16.

41 Watson L and Conway T (1996) *Homes for Independent Living: housing and community care strategies.* Chartered Institute of Housing, Coventry.

42 Camp T (1999) Working together: joint commissioning in practice. *Housing and Support.* 2(1):28–30.

43 Chartered Institute of Housing (1998) *Housing and Health. Good Practice Briefing Issue 13.* CIH, Coventry.

44 Rogers M (1999) Vulnerable tenants in general needs housing. *Housing and Support.* 2(4):8–11.

45 Acheson D (1998) *Inequalities in Health.* HMSO, London.

Chapter 6

The primary care response

Adrian Hastings

Introduction

Doctors and nurses working in primary care must develop an awareness of the multiplicity of factors that influence the health of their patients as individuals, and of the communities where they live. Some of these factors – for example elevated blood pressure – may be unrelated to social circumstances and directly amenable to medical intervention. Others – for example a busy, dangerous road – may result in a great deal of ill health but the solution is not the responsibility of primary care. In future primary care trusts will take on a public health role. Primary care professionals, from their unique role as direct observers of patients' lives and the illnesses which affect them, could encourage primary care trusts to promote policies aimed at reducing health inequalities where these are related to housing and the living environment.

Currently, thinking about housing and health by primary care workers is often limited to dealing with requests for 'a letter for the housing'. Issues about whether the health problem is related to the housing, the impact of the letter on the housing agency and who meets the costs of providing it can result in confrontation between primary care worker and patient. Doctors may think of the impact of housing on health in narrow terms – damp and asthma, arthritis and stairs, depression and tower block living – and be unaware that the evidence for some associations may be weak.[1]

The impact of multiple housing deprivation upon health is much more complex than this and '... would appear to be the same order of magnitude as addressing the issue of smoking, and the risk to health posed by multiple housing deprivation seems to be, on average, greater than that posed by excessive alcohol consumption'.[2] There is a dearth of good research into the impact of improving housing conditions on health, although a prospective trial did establish the value of rehousing on the grounds of mental ill health.[3] Direct proof may be lacking but the circumstantial evidence for the benefits of rehousing is very strong and breaking the link between housing deprivation and health inequalities will depend on retaining a social role for housing policy.[4]

Developing professional awareness

Medical practice is frequently criticised for undue concentration on physical illness and its lack of awareness of the social factors that influence disease. More importantly disease is expressed in individuals with varied psychological make-ups, living in social circumstances that are very different. A heart attack is a physical event – a blood clot blocks an artery and muscle tissue dies. The doctor treating the patient may resignedly attribute the event to poor maternal nutrition when the patient was a foetus, a life-long diet rich in fat and deficient in vegetables, and a two pack per day smoking habit that provides the only morale boosting reward system in his life. However, without an awareness of the relevant causes for each individual seen the management will be deficient and the probability of recurrence greater. Medical education now recognises the importance of the social and behavioural aspects of medicine.[5]

Social and psychological impact of housing on health

Housing is a collective term for all the kinds of buildings in which people dwell. But patients and their families live in homes. The type of home, and a person's feelings towards it, has a profound effect on their psychological and social wellbeing. Despite the focus in research on the physical effects of poor housing, these are more significant for the majority than the creation of physical disease. Primary care workers require an understanding of the types of housing tenure of the populations they serve. For some practices most of their patients live in homes they own, in others local authority-owned premises predominate. Although most attention is given to bad housing, occupied by the poorest in society, even well-to-do people may suffer significant psychological stress if the cost of servicing a mortgage becomes too great. GPs and health visitors recognised the psychological morbidity resulting from the wave of repossessions during the 1990s when interest rates reached their peak. Rent arrears can have a similar effect on tenants and frequently prevent transfers away from areas where they are experiencing problems. They can also impede moves necessary to provide or receive support from other family members, for example to care for a recently disabled elderly parent. Poor relationships between tenants and their landlords (private or public) may contribute to ill health, and disputes with neighbours frequently result in anxiety and depression. These issues may not be presented directly to the doctor or nurse and will require expert consultation skills to reveal them as contributors to the reason for consultation.

Home visiting

GPs, health visitors and district nurses develop considerable insights into the housing circumstances of the populations that they serve when they make visits to patients' homes. With time they develop an awareness of the implication of living in a particular street or maisonette block. The address that new patients give when they register with the practice can tell as much about them as the clothes they wear or the way in which they talk. Primary care health professionals are uniquely placed to understand the links between housing and health. Housing officials and epidemiologists each see half the picture. For doctors and nurses who know their patients' health history, and are invited to visit them in their own homes, this awareness can be essential to the effective management of problems.

Driving to the home one might observe children playing in the street, at risk of accidents and exposed to traffic fumes. Arriving at the maisonette there may be food litter in the entryways attracting rodents and other pests. The stairway may smell of urine, signalling a loss of social solidarity within the community. Graffiti and wanton damage might indicate that young people in the area are bored and disaffected. Within the home the state of decoration and furnishing will reflect the income of the family. If there are children in the household the absence of books and toys can point to an impoverished learning environment. In the home of an elderly person the temperature of different rooms within the house can highlight fuel poverty and climbing a set of steep, narrow stairs to the bedroom flag up the need for adaptations within the home. For individual patients these insights by GPs and health visitors may offer possible solutions by referral to appropriate agencies. There is however a long-term decline in home visiting rates by GPs, which may reduce their sensitivity to these issues.[6]

The institutional response to requests for rehousing

There are many reasons why patients living in social housing seek a move on medical grounds, including conflicts with neighbours, the need to be closer to family, wanting ground-floor accommodation and the need for better amenities. Local authorities use priority-scoring systems for allocating public housing, which are guided by central government.[7] However, the systems vary between authorities resulting in differences in waiting times for families in similar circumstances. Moreover, their efficiency and equity has not been assessed.[8] The methods for eliciting medical evidence in support of these transfers are not standardised and a single practice may have to provide evidence to several different housing associations and local authorities each with its own procedure. Even those with experience in an area may not be familiar with all the procedures.

Patients may present to their doctor saying 'the housing want a letter to state I am ill because of my housing'. Such requests can engender resentment as the nameless official is adding to the pressure on a busy doctor or nurse. The status and effect of such letters is unclear and any fee for the work involved has to be charged to a patient, who is almost certainly living on a very low income. The doctor may believe the letter will be filed, and never acted upon, and it is therefore unlikely that the medical evidence provided will be of sufficient quality to ensure good decision making by the housing provider. Other authorities make written requests using standardised forms which are clear about the information needed and how it will be used. A fee is payable by the housing authority on receipt of the completed document.

There is some evidence of arbitrariness in awarding priority to patients who might benefit from rehousing, with the 'medical points' failing to identify those with needs.[9] It is generally recognised that the current systems for medical priority in rehousing are in need of, and amenable to, improvement.[10] There is concern, however that recent legislation may result in changes, which are administratively cumbersome and result in an inappropriate medicalisation of housing need.[11] Until an equitable and efficient system is introduced, generally health professionals will continue to experience irritation and frustration in their dealings with housing authorities.

Interventions by primary care doctors and nurses

Many patients whose health is affected by their housing will be known to more than one member of the primary care team, although the request will usually be made to one individual. Good practice would suggest that an accurate and effective supporting statement is more likely to be made after consultation between the relevant team members.

Patients may seek help in obtaining support for a modification to a home that is sound, but because of ill health unconnected to the housing, requires adaptation. Examples are the provision of stair lifts after a stroke or the installation of central heating for serious debilitating illness such as multiple sclerosis. Doctors and nurses must be aware of local arrangements for these adaptations to be made when patients cannot afford them, so that the appropriate referral can be made.

Particular problems arise when patients wish to move from housing, which, by its very nature, engenders ill health. An estate can become so dysfunctional that most of its residents wish to move away and seek all possible escape routes – with medical priority one of the most obvious. The housing may be suitable for certain tenants, but not for the people living in it – for example a young family in a tower block flat. The doctor or nurse being asked for support is usually aware that if this patient is successful in moving out, someone with similar circumstances will replace them and the cycle will start again. Recent changes in legislation have provided local authorities with the powers to evict socially disruptive tenants. Consistent use of these powers should address the problem of peaceable people enduring persistent harassment and, in effect, being evicted by their tormentors.

Conclusion

It is necessary to find ways of utilising the understanding of the impact of poor housing upon patients by health professionals in a more equitable way. There is much scope for improving the relationship between primary care and the providers of social housing.[12] The future is likely to hold moves towards closer collaboration between health authorities and local government but the existing relationships are uneasy.[13] The following recommendations are not offered as a complete solution, but if all of them were to be implemented they would go a long way towards meeting the shared aim of health and housing authorities in ensuring that the homes people live in enhance rather than worsen their health.

Recommendations for good practice by housing providers

- Always solicit information from primary care workers in writing, having obtained the client's permission.
- Do not create unrealistic expectations in the mind of your client about the impact of supportive medical evidence.
- Give the name and contact details of the official responsible.
- Specify exactly what information is required about the health of the client and how it will be used in the decisions about adaptations or rehousing.
- Offer a reasonable fee for the work involved.
- Continually review the evidence for the effectiveness of adaptations being provided (e.g. it may be better to provide good ventilation systems with heat exchangers rather than central heating if a client has house-dust mite-induced asthma).
- Employ appropriately trained health professionals – occupational therapists, physiotherapists and doctors – to assess needs and make recommendations.

Recommendations for good practice by primary care workers

- Develop consultation skills so that patients' reasons for consultation are fully established, and the physical, social and psychological contexts are properly explored.
- Ensure effective means of communication between team members so that relevant information is available when responding to housing needs of patients.
- Know how the systems of different housing providers operate – in particular be aware of ineffective measures you may be asked to take.
- Be aware of the referral pathways to access effective help for patients with housing problems.
- Establish systems to review and change practice on a regular basis.

References

1 Hastings A (1975) *The Medical Response to Poor Housing: a report of interviews with 90 Birmingham GPs.* Unpublished.
2 Marsh A, Gordon D, Pantazis C and Heslop P (1999) *Home Sweet Home? The impact of poor housing on health.* Policy Press, Bristol.
3 Elton PJ and Packer JM (1987) Neurotic illness as grounds for medical priority of rehousing. *Public Health.* **101**:233–42.
4 Smith SJ, Alexander A and Easterlow D (1997) Rehousing as a health intervention: miracle or mirage? *Health and Place.* **3**:203–16.
5 General Medical Council (1993) *Tomorrow's Doctors: recommendations on undergraduate medical education.* General Medical Council, London.
6 Aylin P, Majeed AF and Cook DG (1996) Home visiting rates by general practitioners in England and Wales. *BMJ.* **313**:207–10.
7 Secretary of State (1997) *The Allocation of Housing (Procedure)*

Regulations. Department of the Environment, London.

8 Tudor Edwards R (1999) Points for pain: waiting list priority scoring systems. *BMJ.* **318**:412–14.

9 Elton PJ and Packer JM (1986) A prospective randomised trial of the value of rehousing on the grounds of mental ill-health. *J Chronic Dis.* **39**:221–7.

10 Smith SJ, Alexander A and Hill S (1993) *Housing Provision for People with Health and Mobility Needs: guide to good practice for housing managers and health professionals.* Department of Geography, University of Edinburgh, Edinburgh.

11 Connelly J (1996) Housing reform: getting tough on poor people. *BMJ.* **312**:262–3.

12 Easterlow D and Smith SJ (1997) Fit for the future? A role for health professionals in housing management. *Public Health.* **111**:171–8.

13 Hunter DJ (1995) The case for closer cooperation between local authorities and the NHS. *BMJ.* **310**:1587–9.

Chapter 7

Conclusion

Gilles de Wildt, Paramjit S Gill and Iona Heath

Introduction

General practitioners, and other members of the primary care team, are faced regularly with the housing situation of their patients. This adds to knowledge of their patients' individual and social circumstances. In fact, they are probably amongst the very few professionals, which may otherwise include social workers and clergy, who have insight into the private lives and living conditions of a wide variety of people in an increasingly atomised society. This position of being a unique and privileged observer allows primary care professionals to be counsellors and advocates for individuals, as in writing letters of support for rehousing or obtaining improvements on medical grounds. On a collective level it allows health professionals to inform public policy.

Housing is but one determinant of health. Other factors include income, other material conditions, employment, ethnicity, education, social support and psychosocial wellbeing. Hence, GPs and other primary care professionals can only have limited effects. The effect of ethnicity on housing has been highlighted in Chapter 4.

One should caution against expecting too much from primary care and taking attention away from the need for interventions at the level of public health and society as a whole, including action by government and its various departments. Important changes have taken place in the United Kingdom over the last 20 years (*see* Chapter 1). Of relevance here are the widening of the health and income gaps between the richer and the poorer strata of society, the increase in home ownership and the reduction of the social housing stock with an increasing share owned by housing associations at the expense of local government social housing. The role of GPs, however, has not changed significantly.

What is set to change is the organisational structure in which GPs and other members of primary teams operate (*see* Chapters 5 and 6). Primary care trusts are established with lay chairs and social services representatives. There is the possibility for unified budgets between health and social services and primary care trusts are encouraged to work with other government departments and agencies such as housing associations.[1] Also, a number of other initiatives are planned, such as reducing health inequalities within the NHS,[2] the improvement of the social housing stock as detailed in Chapter 1, and improving social and private housing for low income people through the UK Fuel Poverty Strategy.[3]

Against this background, what could be the role of GPs? If there are tasks for GPs and other members of primary care teams, how could they best be defined and supported?

Housing interventions and their effects on health

It is important to understand the relationships between health and housing and the potential roles of primary care professionals. As noted in the previous chapters, these relationships are necessarily complex. Their understanding is hampered by methodological constraints, such as the difficulty of designing and carrying out controlled trials (*see* Chapter 2). There are further conceptual challenges when addressing causal relationships between health, social status, and the relative importance of factors such as income, housing, other material conditions and the psychosocial environment.[4-6] Arguably, housing contains both material and psychosocial aspects.

Naturally, this book cannot be comprehensive. For instance, not included are questions regarding policies to promote the mixing of people of different social backgrounds in one neighbourhood or area and their effects on equity and health. This mixing can be achieved by providing the whole scale of expensive, luxurious, owner-occupied to more austere social housing, as in many cities in the Netherlands and other countries, and also aims to achieve a social mix of children at schools. The latter is achievable in countries where school enrolment depends on geographical vicinity and where private schools which are not subsidised and which require fees, are seen as extreme exceptions, even to parents who can afford it. This situation does not exist at present in the UK. Also not included are questions regarding the effects of crime, perceived sense of security and large-scale arrangements for safe passage of pedestrians and cyclists. These are closely linked with the geography of housing and interact with factors such as social cohesion and social development, and have effects on health, especially of children and the elderly.

Challenges

There are many challenges on the road towards greater equity in health and housing. First, there is the reduction of the social housing stock, while demand remains considerable.

Second, an increasing proportion of the remaining stock is managed by housing associations and other not-for-profit landlords, and a decreasing proportion by local governments. Local government has built up expertise and systems to deal with requests for rehousing on medical grounds, but this often does not extend to housing associations. In spite of guidance, the methods of identifying degrees of priority vary, even between council housing departments. Also, as outlined in Chapter 1, there is a need for clearer government guidance to the non-government social housing sector to rehouse sick and disabled people.

There will remain an important role for GPs and other primary care professionals to provide information to housing authorities. As detailed in Chapter 6, there is, however, an urgent need for simple and effective guidance on the process of identifying the need for rehousing on medical grounds. It is also imperative that the activity of writing a 'letter for the housing' is taken out of the charitable sphere.

Third, as stated before, factors other than those within the direct remit of health services remain of paramount importance, such as improvement of real incomes for poor people, and the availability of good quality social housing in environments which are conducive to advancement. This could include, for instance, the provision of low cost or free nurseries, locally from early morning to late evening, or at work. This would enable poor parents to engage in part-time or full-time work and move out of the poverty trap. Furthermore, the proposed improvements in terms of housing and health require considerable finance, manpower, training and support systems in all sectors concerned. The finances depend on government revenue and expenditure.

Fourth, there are serious shortages of health professionals. Generally speaking, this is most acute in deprived areas.[7] These shortages are unlikely to be relieved in the years to come, while other pressures are mounting, such as increasing attendance rates and increasing workload as a result of national service frameworks[8,9] and defensive medicine to avoid complaints and litigation.[10]

Fifth, as detailed in Chapter 3, the health situation of many homeless people remains poor. The numbers of refugees and asylum seekers have grown. There are serious concerns about their housing conditions and its effect on health, both in terms of physical and social environment. In some instances, as recently observed by an inner-city GP in London, traumatised refugees are crammed into hostels alongside residents with long-standing mental health problems, including psychotic illness, alcohol and drug abuse. Good access to professionals who can deliver adequate primary and mental health care remains problematic.

Sixth, the proposed improvements require systems which identify shortcomings early, and provide feedback to all actors concerned, and to society as a whole, with a view to facilitating open and informed debate about policy choices. Deficiencies could include substandard housing improvements and substandard care from health and social service providers. Another block could be the mismatch between unrealistic targets and demands and the lack of front-line capacity to deliver. This can lead to the creation of virtual realities, as has often been the case in the NHS and other government sectors.[11,12] To counteract this, there is a need for an independent health inspectorate. Independence and openness could be secured by a statutory position comparable with that of the National Audit Office. It is not certain that the Commission for Health Improvement can play this role while questions about its general direction remain.[13]

Seventh, questions remain regarding potentially conflicting government initiatives. The role of private finance initiatives in the NHS is increasing[14] and practices in trade are changing as a result of economic globalisation and rules of the World Trade Organisation. There is a concern that the ability to develop and implement equitable public health policies, including policies which relate to housing, can be undermined by the nature and role of for-profit providers.[15]

Opportunities

Opportunities will arise for GPs and other primary care professionals, such as health visitors, practice nurses and district nurses. The government acknowledges the role of housing for health, as shown in initiatives such as the fuel poverty strategy.[3] Primary care trusts with GPs and others on their Boards will be expected to help deliver local Health Improvement Programmes, which may incorporate collaboration with other government departments and non-government agencies, including the housing area.[1] Primary care professionals may optimise their limited but essential role in providing information for medical priority rehousing by helping to develop intersectoral guidelines on good practice. Guidelines need to be based on a mix of national standards, local population needs and the ways in which primary care trusts, social services and housing departments operate in defined geographical areas. The role of primary care professionals as observers and narrators of people's lives and housing conditions remains important for informing public policy, including feedback on progress and blocks.

Opportunities exist to improve care to the homeless, including hostel dwellers. While local governments and other agencies, spurred by the Rough Sleepers Unit, have managed to reduce the numbers of rough sleepers in the UK,[16] there is still a long way to go in addressing issues of prevention and reintegration into society. Serious problems exist of access to adequate primary and mental health care. Many homeless people move address frequently – from B&B to hostel to the street – and lead a chaotic lifestyle. They often have the greatest health needs. For them the best way forward may be the provision of properly resourced specialist primary and mental health care services, which offer help early and guide patients into mainstream care. Primary care trusts, if properly guided and resourced, will have the ability to collaborate with other government and non-government agencies, and may offer an effective framework to facilitate improved health and social care to homeless people.

References

1 NHS Executive (2001) *Shifting the Balance of Power Within the NHS: securing delivery.* Consultation document. NHSE, Leeds.
2 Department of Health (2001) *Tackling Health Deliveries. Consultation of a plan for delivery.* DoH, London.
3 Department of the Environment, Transport and the Regions (2001) *The UK Fuel Poverty Strategy.* Consultation draft. HMSO, London.
4 Lynch JW, Davey Smith G, Kaplan G and House JS (2000) Income equality and mortality: importance to health of individual income, psychological environment, or material conditions. *BMJ.* **320**:1200–4.
5 Lynch JW, Due P, Muntaner C and Davey Smith G (2000) Social

capital: is it a good investment strategy for public health? *J Epidemiol Comm Health.* **54**:404–8.

6 Wilkinson R (2000) Inequality and the social environment: a reply to Lynch *et al. J Epidemiol Comm Health.* **54**:411–13.

7 Hasting A and Rao M (2001) Doctoring deprived areas cannot rely on exceptional people. *BMJ.* **323**:409–10.

8 Hippisley-Cox J and Pringle M (2001) General practice workload implications of the national service framework for coronary heart disease: cross sectional survey. *BMJ.* **323**:269–70.

9 McManus R, Lumley L, Gough M *et al.* (2001) Framework will have considerable effect on primary care. *BMJ.* **323**:337.

10 Barton A (2001) Medical litigation: who benefits? *BMJ.* **322**:1189.

11 Jones J (2000) The secret life of the NHS. *BMJ.* **320**:1457–9.

12 Salter B (1998) Virtual politics in the new NHS. *BMJ.* **317**:1091.

13 Day P and Klein R (2001) Commission for Health Improvement invents itself. It needs to decide whether it is the quality police or a midwife of change. *BMJ.* **322**:1502–3.

14 Pollock A (2001) Will primary care trusts lead to US style healthcare? *BMJ.* **322**:964–7.

15 Pollock A, Player S and Godden S (2001) How corporate finance is moving primary care into corporate ownership. *BMJ.* **322**:960–3.

16 Department of Transport, Local Government and the Regions (2001) *Rough Sleepers Unit. Coming in from the cold. Progress report on the Government's strategy on rough sleeping.* DTLGR, London.

Index

Acheson inquiry into health
inequalities 93–4
adaptation, local authority assistance
for 6
adults, research on 32
Afghans *see* ethnic minorities
African-Caribbeans *see* ethnic
minorities
age 83
see also children; older people;
young people
homelessness and 51
vulnerable people 83
area-based (ecological) studies 18
Asians *see* ethnic minorities
asthma
children 7, 22–3, 32
damp housing 22
asylum seekers 47, 70, 83, 112
atopy 22
Audit Commission report on role of
housing in community care 85

Bangladeshis *see* ethnic minorities
black and minority ethnic (BME)
groups *see* ethnic minorities
Bosnians *see* ethnic minorities
Building Regulations 5

care needs, ethnic minorities 75
Caribbeans *see* ethnic minorities
caring communities 90
Caring for People 83
Centre for Housing Policy 51
chain migration, ethnic minorities 69
challenges 111–13
CHI (Commission for Health
Improvement) 113

children
asthma 7, 22–3, 32
wheezing 34
Chinese *see* ethnic minorities
cold
excess winter deaths 33–4
health implications 33–4
mental health and 36
physical effects 19
research rationale 21
collaboration 79–80
inter-agency projects 91–3
issues 84–7
joint planning and commissioning
88–90
housing provision and
management 80–2
multi-agency programmes 90–1
opportunities 87–8
vulnerable people 83–4
combustion products of fuel 19
Commission for Health Improvement
(CHI) 113
commissioning, joint 88–90
community care 4, 83, 85
concealed households, ethnic
minorities 73
council housing *see* social housing
crowding *see* overcrowding

damp
cold, producing 20
mental health and 36
mould 22–3
research 21, 22–3, 32
deaths
excess winter 33–4
rough sleepers 55

demographic details
  homelessness *see* homelessness
'deserving poor' 50
determinants of health 109
disabled people
  ethnic minorities 72
  housing related issues 92
  integration 90
  ordinary housing 81
Disabled Persons Housing Service
  (DPHS) 92
discrimination, racial 68
drug abuse and homelessness 54–5

East African Asians *see* ethnic
  minorities
ecological studies 18
eczema 22
elderly people *see* older people
energy efficiency 20
English House Condition Survey
  72
epidemiological enquiries 19–20
epidemiological studies of housing
  and health 24–31
ethnic minorities 67
  care needs, assessment of 75
  chain migration 69
  concealed households 73
  disabled people 72
  extended families, break-up 71–2
  GPs, implications for 75–6
  healthcare providers, implications
    for 75–6
  homelessness 51–2, 73
  household types 71–2
  housing tenure and amenities
    72–5
  human rights 75
  language support 75–6
  migration 70
  numbers 67–70
  overcrowding 73
  owner occupation 72
  primary care, implications for 75–6

  privately rented housing 72
  racial discrimination 68
  refugees 70
  social housing 72
  social services support 74
  settlement patterns 67–70
  suburbanisation 68
evidence base 37
excess winter deaths 33–4
extended families, break-up 71–2

families, extended, break-up 71–2
fibrinogen 34
Fitness for Human Habitation
  standard 6
formaldehyde 19
fuel combustion products 19
fungi 22
  see also mould

General Health Questionnaire (GHQ)
  36
general practitioners
  ethnic minorities implications for
    75–6
  homeless people registration with
    56–7
GHQ (General Health Questionnaire)
  36
good practice
  housing providers,
    recommendations for 105
  primary care workers,
    recommendations for 106
government
  collaboration policies and
    initiatives 86, 87–8
  conflicting initiatives 113
  public health function 4
  public spending reductions 81–2
  Social Exclusion Unit 90
GPs *see* general practitioners
Griffiths Report 83
group maintenance schemes 8
Gujaratis *see* ethnic minorities

handypersons' schemes 8
HAZs *see* health action zones
health
  consequences, housing conditions
    and 17–45
  determinants 109
  homelessness and 52–5
  housing interventions effects on
    110–11
  and income, gaps 109
  psychological impact of housing on
    101
  relevance of housing policy to 5–8
  social impact of housing on 101
  socio-economic status and,
    association between 74
health action zones (HAZs) 4, 80, 86,
  90–1
health authorities
  local authorities and, collaboration
    88–9
health impact assessments (HIAs) 4
health improvement programmes
  (HImPs) 4, 80, 89, 113
Health Improvement Programmes:
  planning for better health and
  better health care 89
health inequalities, Acheson inquiry
  into 93–4
health inspectorate, independent 113
Health of the Nation 3, 80
health policy
  relevance of housing to 3–4
health professionals, shortages of 112
health services
  social housing allocation roles 93
healthcare providers
  ethnic minorities implications for
    75–6
healthy housing
  markets 10–12
  quest for 2–8
HIAs (health impact assessments) 4
HImPs *see* health improvement
  programmes

Home Energy Efficiency Scheme 6–7
home improvement, repair and
  adaptation
  local authority assistance for 6
home maintenance initiatives 7–8
home ownership *see* owner
  occupation
home visiting, primary care 101–2
homelessness 83, 112, 114
  age and 51
  causes 49–50
  centres 58–9
  definitions 47–8
  demographic details
    official or statutory homeless
      population 50–1
    unofficial or non-statutory
      homeless population 51–2
  describing 50
  drug abuse 54–5
  ethnic minorities 51–2, 73
  health and 52–5
  measuring 48–9
  mental health 54
  poor health
    as cause of homelessness 54–5
    homelessness as cause of 53
    homelessness as exacerbating
      factor of 53
  primary care for homeless people
    current service provision 57–8
    evaluation criteria *58*
    future 60–1
    integrated services 59–60
    registration with GPs 56–7
    separate or specialised services
      58–9
  rough sleepers *see* rough sleepers
  standardised morbidity rates
    (SMR) of homeless people 55,
    56
  trauma 53
  tuberculosis 53
  young people 52
homes 101

hospitals 83
    inter-agency projects involving
        discharges or admissions 91–2
house-dust mites 19, 21–2, 32
household types
    ethnic minorities 71–2
housing
    marginalisation 88
    psychological impact on health 101
    relevance to health policy 3–4
    social impact on health 101
Housing and Community Care 83–4
housing associations 10, 110, 111
    special needs provisions 81
housing authorities
    information from primary care 111
housing conditions and health
    consequences 17–45
Housing Corporation 5
housing for health *see* housing policy
Housing Health and Safety Rating
    Scheme 6
housing interventions, effects on
    health 110–11
housing management, collaboration
    80–2
housing markets, healthy 10–12
housing needs
    joint approaches to assessment 89
housing policy 1–2, 79
    Centre for Housing Policy 51
    housing for health 8–9
        healthy housing markets 10–12
        medical priority rehousing
            (MPR) 9–10
        quest for healthy housing 2–8
        relevance of housing to health
            policy 3–4
        relevance to health 5–8
housing providers
    recommendations for good
        practice by 105
housing provision, collaboration 80–2
housing related issues, disabled
    people 92

housing tenure and amenities
    ethnic minorities 72–5
human rights, ethnic minorities 75
hypertension 34
hypothermia 33

income gap 109
independent health inspectorate 113
Indians *see* ethnic minorities
integrated primary care services for
    homeless people 59–60
integration of disabled people 90
*Integration of Joint Finance Allocation
    1999/2000*: 88
inter-agency projects 91–3
interdisciplinary teams 91
internal environment studies 19–20
interventions by primary care 104
ischaemic heart disease 34

joint funding arrangements 4
joint planning and commissioning
    88–90

Kurds *see* ethnic minorities

language support, ethnic minorities
    75–6
'letters for the housing' 99, 103, 112
lifetime homes 81
    standards 5
local authorities
    assistance for home improvement,
        repair and adaptation 6
    financial assistance for owner
        occupiers 12
    health authorities and,
        collaboration 88–9
    independence of departments 86
    modernisation 86–7
    priority-scoring systems 103
    sale of social housing 82
    spending restrictions 82
    transfer of housing stock to social
        housing organisations 10

Major Repairs Allowance 7
marginalisation of housing 88
measuring homelessness 48–9
medical assessments for rehousing 93
medical priority rehousing (MPR)
    9–10
mental health 34–6, 83
  homelessness 54
migration, ethnic minorities 70
Minister for Public Health 4
minority ethnic groups *see* ethnic
    minorities
modernisation of local authorities
    86–7
mortality *see* deaths
mould 19, 22, 23, 32
MPR (medical priority rehousing)
    9–10
multi-agency programmes 90–1
mycotoxins 22

New Deal for Regeneration
    programme 90
The New NHS: modern, dependable 89
noise 35–6
numbers of ethnic minorities 67–70
nurse practitioners
  homeless people 61

older people
  hypothermia 33
  inter-agency projects 92
opportunities 113–14
ordinary housing, disabled people 81
Our Healthier Nation 80
overcrowding 20, 35
  ethnic minorities 73
owner occupation 11
  ethnic minorities 72
  increase in 109–10
  local authorities financial assistance
      for 12

Pakistanis *see* ethnic minorities
Partners in Action 88

partnership approach 4
pathogens 19
PCT *see* primary care trusts
Personal Medical Services (PMS)
    pilots
  homeless people 58–9, 60
PFI (Private Finance Initiative) 7
planning, joint 88–90
PMS *see* Personal Medical Services
    pilots
pollutants 19
poor health
  homelessness *see* homelessness
primary care
  ethnic minorities implications for
      75–6
  home visiting 101–2
  for homeless people *see*
      homelessness
  implications 37–8
  information to housing authorities
      111
  interventions 104
  professional awareness of social
      factors, developing 100
  recommendations for good
      practice by 106
  response 99–107
primary care trusts (PCTs) 80, 110
  homeless people 60
  opportunities 113–14
priority-scoring systems 103
Private Finance Initiative (PFI) 7
privately rented housing
  ethnic minorities 72
professional awareness of social
    factors
  primary care developing 100
psychological impact of housing on
    health 101
public health
  government function 4
  initiatives 2
  White Paper 5
public spending reductions 81–2

Punjabis *see* ethnic minorities

racial discrimination 68
radon 19
refugees 70, 83, 112
registered social landlords (RSL) 5
rehousing 35, 111–12
    institutional response to requests
        for 102–3
    medical assessments for 93
    medical priority (MPR) 9–10
repairs
    local authority assistance for 6
    on prescription 7
research on housing and health 18–36
resettlement teams 92
residential care 82, 83
respiratory health 32
rough sleepers 48, 49, 51–2, 55, 114
RSL (registered social landlords) 5

Saving Lives: Our Healthier Nation 3,
    5
separate primary care services for
    homeless people 58–9
settlement patterns, ethnic minorities
    67–70
sheltered housing 80–1
Single Regeneration Budget 86
sleeping rough *see* rough sleepers
slum clearances 2
SMR *see* standardised morbidity rates
social context of housing 20–2
Social Exclusion Unit 90
social factors, professional awareness
    of primary care developing 100
social housing 7
    ethnic minorities 72
    health services allocation roles 93
    reduction of stock 110, 111
    sale by local authorities 82
    special schemes 80–1

social housing organisations
    local authorities transfer of housing
        stock to 10
social impact of housing on health
    101
social services
    ethnic minorities, support for 74
socio-economic status
    health and, association between 74
Somalis *see* ethnic minorities
South Asians *see* ethnic minorities
special schemes, social housing 80–1
specialised primary care services for
    homeless people 58–9
standardised morbidity rates (SMR)
    homeless people 55, *56*
suburbanisation, ethnic minorities 68
*Supporting People: A new policy and
    funding framework for support
    services* 89
Supporting People programme 4
Survey of English Housing 1994/5:
    50–1

temperatures 19
    see also cold
trauma 53
travellers 83
tuberculosis 53

'undeserving poor' 50

virtual realities 113
volatile organic compounds (VOC)
    19
vulnerable people, collaboration 83–4

West Indians *see* ethnic minorities
wheezing 34
winter deaths 33–4

young people, homelessness 52